Praise for RAISING OWEN

This book was so relatable to me from the beginning to the end. It was fascinating reading about the trail she blazed for inclusion, not just for her son, but for all of us! It is a beautifully written book that takes us along on her journey of raising an amazing son.

Anne L., Texas

I found the book so deeply thoughtful, honest and personal. The vulnerable way the author articulated her story would resonate with anyone going through something unexpected. An emotional juggling of heartache, joy and surprise leading up to a story of unconditional love. Just wonderful!

Angela M., California

Raising Owen is an uplifting story of one mother's journey. It draws you in to the daily joys and struggles of raising a child with Down Syndrome, but is meaningful to any parent raising a child with differences. In her journey, Suzanne lifts herself, her family, and her community along the way.

Laura W., Michigan

Raising Owen

Raising Owen

An extra-ordinary memoir on motherhood

Suzanne Lezotte

Aristata Press

Raising Owen: An Extra-Ordinary Memoir on Motherhood
Copyright © 2023 by Suzanne Lezotte

All rights reserved. No portion of this book may be reproduced, stored in a retrieval system, or transmitted in any form or by any means—electronic, mechanical, photocopy, recording, scanning, or other—except for brief quotations in critical reviews or articles, without the prior written permission of the publisher.

Library of Congress Control Number: 2023939142

This work depicts actual events in the life of the author as truthfully as recollection permits and/or can be verified by research. Occasionally, dialogue consistent with the character or nature of the person speaking has been supplemented. All persons within are actual individuals; there are no composite characters. The names of some individuals have been changed to respect their privacy.

ISBN: 979-8-9878524-3-9 (hardcover)
ISBN: 979-8-9878524-2-2 (paperback)
ISBN: 979-8-9878524-4-6 (ebook)

Cover design by Lisa Thomas, LCT Studio, Inc.

Aristata Press, Portland, Oregon

To my husband, Erik: for always believing in me
To my son, Owen: the best subject I could ever hope for
To Tess and Axel: for keeping it real

"The difference between ordinary and extraordinary is that little extra."

Jimmy Johnson

Introduction

I wrote this book to honor the perseverance of parents: how we will fight for our child no matter who they are, who they become, or what challenges arise. This is my journey as a parent, and mine alone. Nobody's path looks the same. Yet we can still find similarities in the growth that defines us, the lessons we learned, and the innate fascination of watching a human being unfold.

I didn't know my oldest son, Owen, would have Down syndrome before he was born, as many parents do. When doctors diagnosed him at seven days old, I was blindsided, to say the least. I had been eagerly awaiting bringing Owen home from the NICU; watching my world crumble after his unexpected diagnosis was not in the game plan. His fate seemed sealed with a gloomy future that included heart problems, vision issues, physical and cognitive delays, dental complications, and the inability to live and process life as a typical child. At least, that's what the doctors told me. Never once did I hear a doctor say, "Rest assured, your child will be kind," or "He will be wickedly funny," or "His love will extend for miles." Doctors don't tell you those things. Maybe it's because kindness, humor, and love in those with Down syndrome haven't yet been proven scientifically.

Owen taught me far more lessons than I bargained for. He

taught me about patience and miracles. He taught his siblings about empathy and gratitude. He taught strangers about laughter and fortitude. Still, my experience did not always embody beautiful, glowing happiness. I cried during much of Owen's first year. Why? Because society's idea of what a Down syndrome diagnosis looks like was deeply ingrained in me. I was crying over how I thought he should have been born. I robbed myself (and him) of so many beautiful hours because it took me a while to accept his diagnosis. And yet, as with any undesirable diagnosis, the stages of grief must be acknowledged and hurdled. Owen was not born the child I thought he would be (and in a brilliant flash of hindsight, I realized neither were my two neurotypical kids). I not only grieved the ideal of who I thought Owen should be, I grieved for myself. I had to surrender the person I'd come to be until this point in my life and transform into something . . . unknown. The first thing I surrendered was releasing my firmly placed expectations of having a child who would require a different life map than I'd drawn. I had to prepare myself for and welcome in the new experiences that would arise on the road I'd started down. The second thing I surrendered was the notion that Owen got the raw end of the deal with this diagnosis. Who was I to say what was best for him, our family, and all who he would come in contact with throughout his life? As I waded through memories and stories, I realized this book was not only about my journey of self-introspection and lessons learned along the way. This book showcased the self-actualization of my son and his abilities through our push for inclusion.

A few months ago, I pondered the question I hear a lot from parents who have a child with a disability about to enter the school system: "Will my child get bullied?" Parents ask this heartfelt question based on their fears and lack of understanding. I smile as I tell them the story about Anthony. You see, Anthony was a child who Owen described as "the boy who saved my life" after an incident in middle school. As I was driving Owen home one afternoon, he spoke in almost a whisper to tell me that someone had bullied him at school the day before. I nearly pulled over in the middle of traffic, aghast that he had waited so long to tell me. Also, I wondered if it had happened before. As the story unfolded, he recounted sitting in the locker room on the bench changing clothes when another boy started yelling at him to get up and move. Apparently, Owen was sitting directly in front of this boy's locker. Displaying his own unique brand of courage, my son didn't want to move, so he shook his head without uttering a word. This boy, who happened to be in the cadet program at the school, began yelling at Owen, and some of the other cadets shuffled over, forming a circle around him, joining in on the threats. An eighth-grader entered the locker room and promptly interrupted the melee, disbanding the boys. He asked Owen if he was okay and introduced himself as Anthony. Arriving home, I called the school and they immediately addressed the situation.

My heart ached for Owen; I felt as if I had let him down. I questioned whether we should have done what other parents did: have him already dressed for PE so he didn't have to go into the locker room. But I wanted him to be included the same way other kids were, and that meant (per our insistence in his IEP) he had to change clothes in the locker room. After all, we had already set a precedent by teaching him to navigate the locker room at his swim meets, which were often on a college campus, and I couldn't go in there with him.

The next morning, while rushing the kids out the door for school, I quickly grabbed a thank-you card from my drawer and hurriedly penned a note: *Dear Anthony, my son Owen calls you "the boy who saved my life." I've never met you, but I wanted to thank you for standing up for him. Not everyone would have done what you did. I am again reminded that the right people will find my son and champion him.*

I sealed the note and told Owen to make sure and give it to Anthony. The next day, Owen told me that the school held an assembly on bullying and honored Anthony for stepping in. With a smile and sigh, I knew my work was done.

A few days later, my son's teacher sent me an email with an embedded video. "Is this you, Rockstar Mom?" she wrote. I opened the link to see a news story on bullying, and my note was on the screen. Tears came to my eyes when I realized how this incident had unfolded and became a teaching moment for so many of us in Owen's universe.

Fast-forward to a few months ago (five years have elapsed since this incident) and Owen tells me that Anthony is coming for a visit. I am surprised. I knew they stayed in touch, but most of the neurotypical friends he made along the way seemed to drop off after high school graduation. Anthony drove an hour to see us, and as the boys were chilling in the living room, he mentioned he wanted to share a story. He explained that during his senior year of high school, his teacher gave the students an extra-credit project to bring up their grades. The assignment was to write an essay about a time where you stood up for something you believed in. After he turned in the essay, his teacher submitted the students' essays for a school contest. Anthony's essay won first prize. Then it was submitted regionally. Again, Anthony took first place. When his essay reached the state competition, he was invited to Palm Springs for an awards ceremony. As he entered the ballroom, he was told he won first prize and was asked to read his essay. The essay was about the scenario with Owen, and my letter was up on the screen. As he told this story, I was reminded again of not only the empathy that we all have for one another, but the ways in which my son has touched others and continues to connect with their hearts. Much like how a stone dropped in a pond produces far-reaching ripples, Owen's spirit continues to oh-so-gently nudge others' hearts, thus changing outcomes from fear to love, from chaos to calm, from rejection to acceptance.

That message is what I want you to walk away with after reading this book. We all have an effect on each other, no matter what our disability or ability may be. Nobody can predict how magnificent your child will be. Only you can determine what that is by the lens through which you view your story.

Chapter One

The regretful word slipped out of my mouth before I could catch it. Before I could prevent piercing the soul of my child, who didn't yet grasp the burden of frustration or fully understand its meaning. Or did he? He was still a child in my mind, even as the wiry hairs sprouting on his chin indicated an emerging manhood that filtered through the lines of his body. He sat next to me, his round eyes a murky hazel and his eyelashes blinking rapidly. These facial cues always came moments before a well of tears sprang forth.

It was springtime, and the housing market was booming. My husband, Erik, and I had chosen to put our house on the market—a decision not made lightly. Situated on a corner lot, ours was a favorite location for the neighborhood kids to play hide-and-seek. A milestone moment for parents who held their tiny toddlers' hands as they mastered the three steps to our front door. A destination for selfies when the Halloween ghosts appeared or the Christmas cow graced our lawn. During the summer, the birds of paradise seemed to chat with our lemon tree as it bowed beneath its fragrant harvest. Over the sixteen years we lived there, our house welcomed three kids, one dog, one cat, two rats, and an insane sensibility that our lives were one big, messy puzzle in which all the pieces miraculously fit together. Neither Erik nor I knew anything about raising a child with a disability, nor, in fact about raising kids in general. Somehow, we made it all work. But we had reached a point where we wanted to move to a smaller town that offered better schools. Mainly, though, we were ready to mix it all up again.

Erik insisted we involve our teenagers in the decision, and I bristled at getting their input. I grew up one of nine kids, and my parents never involved us in any of their big decisions. My father was an electrician, and none of us were aware of his income, how big the mortgage was (if our parents even had one!), or how they managed to feed nine hungry mouths. My resistance to change forced me look inward. Why not involve them? From Erik's perspective, perhaps this was the start of our kids collectively sharing responsibilities, learning life skills, and taking the first steps toward independence.

It was on this day we received a call to show our house with very little time to vacate, and I'd hoped to slip out the back door as the potential buyers came through the front. Hastening the kids out the door, our dog sensed the excitement and eagerly leapt into the chaos as I barked my commands to the kids to get moving.

"Don't let Shaggy out the door just yet!" I yelled, hands grasping my purse, my phone, errant water bottles, and as many snacks as I could find in the kitchen. I stepped onto the patio and watched as my oldest son, Owen, partially opened the gate. Sensing his freedom, Shaggy pushed between Owen and the door and nosed it fully open, then ran toward the street.

"Owen! Why are you so _____?" I screamed frustratedly. And the word I had raised my kids to believe was so terrible—akin to the worst swear word anyone could say—effortlessly rolled out. Almost as if time slowed, I saw the word unfurl from my mouth in incremental seconds: *Stuuu-piddd*. Yes, I said it. I told my son with Down syndrome he was stupid.

My daughter, Tess, glared at me. "Any one of us could have made that mistake," she pointed out flatly. "Not just Owen." She turned and reached for his arm ever so gently, locking it with hers, and they walked side by side to the car. Shaggy had reached the end of the driveway, and I grabbed him, desperate to get him contained. He'd had so many escape-artist moments over the years, with negative results to both him, others, and our family. My thoughts flashed back to when he ran out and threatened a passerby with bared teeth and a low growl, his appearance a cross between Doberman and German Shepherd, which would be frightening for anyone. So many apologies were given to neighbors and friends, assuring them he wasn't a bad dog; he was just being protective. Every day he perched on the couch in the living room, his eyes watchful, his bark beginning as a low rumble, the full force of it directed at the dogs who pranced onto our lawn and marked a spot, arrogantly glancing his way. All day long he raced from the front door to the back door with an incessant bark that hurt my ears. I was on constant alert when the mailman came. Any delivery person who came close to our door and heard Shaggy's bark immediately left the package and sprinted back to their truck rather than wait for the required signature.

At the car, the kids were silent as they piled in. Shaggy was wild, unwilling to jump in until I lifted his legs and he was forced to climb in, as if he knew change was brewing. Slowly driving away, I watched as a couple entered our house, lovingly holding hands. The woman shot the man an understanding glance as if just catching his joke, then threw her head back in laughter.

As I drove around the neighborhood, my stomach curdled, and the tension in the car was palpable. Owen wouldn't look at me, and my shame made it unbearable to look at him lest I glimpse a painful reflection of myself in his eyes. I circled the neighborhood again, having no intended destination, until finally coming to a stop at the park near our house. This house showing could take fifteen minutes or an hour, depending on how interested the couple was.

My daughter finally broke the silence. "You're so busy posting how much you love Owen on Facebook, but maybe you should tell everybody what you really think of him." Her tone was defiant, and I fought back tears as her chastening echoed through my soul.

"I guess this is a lesson to you that not everybody's life is perfect on social media, including mine!" I retorted. More silence ensued.

I glanced at Owen, not sure how to repair my destructive mistake, so I started with the words I knew he needed to hear.

"I'm sorry, Owen. I'm so sorry. I didn't mean to call you *that*." His eyes began to blink faster, and even as I knew he was going to cry, he valiantly tried to hold in his tears.

"You always say things . . ." His words trailed off, and I cringed at what he'd not said but felt. I knew he meant to say, ". . . like *that*." I had actually never used the s-word in relation to Owen before, but I frequently acted annoyed or frustrated, urging him to hurry up, to stop getting distracted, and to move faster. The word *slow* came to my mind often, and even though I never said he was slow, I wondered if he knew that word lived in my unspoken language. Owen was so intuitive. My tone was constantly on the verge of yelling, as if by raising my voice he would heed what I was asking. I hadn't realized he was listening to my tonal cues and internalizing them as much as my other kids did. Big, fat tears started to squeeze out of his eyes, then slowly slid down his face.

"Owen, please know that I didn't mean to call you *that word*. I was trying to make sure Shaggy didn't get out and hurt anyone."

"He wouldn't hurt anyone, Mom," Owen assured me, his shoulders rising and falling with each wave of a sob. He cried hard for a moment as he always did, but the storm was sure to lift—as it always did. I thought of his response to me and how he seemed to inherently understand our dog more than I did. My unease came from the few times Shaggy had come dangerously close to nipping at our friends. These same friends were now verifiably terrified when they showed up to our house. Owen looked at me, but there was no anger or judgment evident, only a deep well of truth radiating from his eyes.

"I love you, Mom," he said. Immediately, the shame I felt was now bathed by the glow of his unfiltered love. I was once again reminded of Owen's inability to hate or hold a grudge. I knew I would be the bearer of my own guilt for crossing the line that I had always set for myself, not my son. The regretful word was on a loop in my brain, and I didn't know how to make it up to him, or to any of my kids. I recalled my childhood memories, certain that among the echoing voices of parents, peers, and siblings, I had been called stupid at some point too. "Hurt people hurt people" was a phrase I'd read recently, and it had stuck in my mind ever since. I knew I was perpetuating the same cycle of childhood trauma. I recall having a sense of how tough my growing-up years must have been for my mom, who, while raising nine kids, constantly refereed fights between the siblings, planned and prepared meals daily, purchased clothes and shoes while sacrificing new threads for herself because we grew like weeds, and made certain we stayed in school. How had she gotten through it? And how was I failing so badly with my tribe of three? Perhaps I was finally experiencing the humility that inevitably occurs while raising kids. I thought I was good at it—even better than some—but at the end of the day, I was no better than my worst moment of parenting.

I didn't dare tell anyone about my parenting fail until a week later, when I spoke candidly with my friend Jen, whose daughter, Ava, also has Down syndrome. Owen and Ava had created a special bond over the years, and we had planned a date to meet up. Jen and I spoke quietly a short distance away from them as they chatted. My bottled-up confession came pouring out, and I felt the searing shame pierce me again as I told her what happened. She looked at me with no judgment.

"Don't worry," she said conspiratorially. "I've said it too. Do you know why though?" She paused but I didn't answer. I needed to hear her confession in order to feel somewhat human again. "Because we expect Owen and Ava to know better. We are not giving them a hall pass because they have Down syndrome. You're not the first parent to say something you regret to your child, and you won't be the last."

I chewed on her words for a moment as I watched the afternoon breeze ruffle my son's hair, his smile cajoling a conversation out of Ava as she preened in her new bathing suit. I knew my choice of words was wrong—that was apparent—but Jen was right. I expected Owen to know better—not just in that harried moment before the house showing, but in other situations too. I inherently knew he was smart. Although Owen didn't deserve the overly reactive verbal berating I dished out, I was sure that he was aware of appropriate actions and did know better.

I often think of the early days when my son was a newborn. Being my first, it was like Christmas morning every day. I couldn't wait to wake up and snuggle his tiny limbs, kiss his round, pudgy face, and watch his eyes roam the room, searching for invisible delights that made him point at the ceiling. I had a theory that he was watching spiritual beings as he laughed and clapped. One time, he fixed his gaze intently on a bottle of wine as I slowly poured a glass. Erik and I joked that he was an old soul who had lived during the Renaissance, eating and drinking among the royalty. Maybe I wasn't far off. Owen was my prince, and he would grow into a king one day. Every night for many years I told him as much when I knelt by his bed, watching his body morph from a baby into a toddler. He always fought sleep, and I recall hearing the click of his pacifier as he sucked it vigorously to soothe himself. When his breath slowed, the pacifier would fall out of his mouth and he'd lay there, arms flung straight out as if he were waiting to receive a blessing. Those nights I prayed over him as he drifted off, halfway between wakefulness and sleep, my words were both a fervent prayer to him and to God.

"You are going to do great things one day, Owen," I'd whispered over and over. "You will change the way people think." Little did I know the peaks and valleys I would go through to arrive at the very same conclusion as he rounded the curve into adulthood.

Chapter Two

I don't exactly know when I started to believe in serendipity, or even pay attention to the phenomena, but so much about life in general is due to timing. For me, this story needs to begin when I met my husband. If I hadn't met him and we hadn't gotten married and had a child, I would not be writing this particular story. As such, this is a story of love, despair, truth, beauty, and magic, which is what all of our stories are about, strung together with stardust and moonbeams.

The story Erik likes to tell is that he crashed a party my friends and I were hosting. Later that night, when he confessed to said infiltration, I couldn't resist his boldness and charm and thus kissed him. It took us many years—seven to be exact—of dating, then not dating, before we finally committed to marriage. I like to tell the story differently though. My version reveals how the universe conspired to bring us together, thereby paving the way for us to join our lives and create the beautiful family that we have today.

That year, Halloween fell on a Saturday night, which happens about once every six years, adjusting for leap year. I lived in the Hollywood Hills in an old building on Cheremoya Street—reminiscent of 1920s Spanish architecture—that shared a courtyard with my neighbors. Initially, everyone wanted to throw a party on

Halloween. Unfortunately, it was the one year that an organization I worked with changed their annual awards event to October. Even worse, they moved it to Saturday night, so I had to work on Halloween night. Collectively, we decided to postpone our party one week and dubbed it the "After Halloween Party."

In a parallel world, the man who would become my husband was at a party up the street from my apartment on Halloween. If we'd had our party that same night, we never would have met. It was his birthday, after all, and the perfect excuse to throw a party. But the following weekend Erik and his friends, while sitting in their house in The Hills, heard the band that was practicing. Our friends who lived downstairs were in a band, and they jumped at the chance to play at the party.

"If you can hear the music, you're invited," Erik announced to his friends, boredom apparent among them. Up for any adventure, they drove down the hill, parked, and wandered in. Late in the night, when almost everyone had gone, Erik and I sat on the steps and he admitted they'd crashed the party. Instinctively, I kissed him. From that night on, we dated on and off for a while, neither one of us willing to admit we wanted to be "together," but together enough for everyone to assume we were. In my mind, I knew I was going to marry him. It was that simple.

Erik's family invested in and built homes, and when I met him, he was out of work. He surprised me one night by admitting that he was impressed how I picked up my life and moved from Michigan to LA. For Erik, it was incomprehensible to him to leave the world he grew up in and start over in someplace unknown. I was so hungry to succeed, to make a name for myself, that I frequently focused on my failures, pushing myself to do better and work harder. The confidence he had in himself was alluring; I had never known that kind of person. In quick succession, he bought a house in the Hollywood Hills and then helped me find one to buy. We lived one address number off, on a hill that wound its way down the mountain. When we got married, we pooled our resources from the sale of my house and the rental of his and purchased one together. We were finding shared success and happiness. We moved into a 1930s Spanish-style house in the

Hollywood Hills off the Cahuenga Pass, and not long after I became pregnant with Owen. I was sure this house had its own ghost, but nothing frightened me when I was home. Interestingly, it proved to be a personal spiritual womb I sought refuge in when the world tilted and unleashed its chaos.

Parenting doesn't necessarily require training, yet I was conditioned to believe I could do it. All those years of babysitting gave me the confidence to believe I could handle any baby, toddler, or child. Yet a niggling doubt began arise. What if I dragged all my baggage and fears with me? What if my issues transferred to my son? I pushed the negative thoughts aside, latching on to the same fire that drove me to Los Angeles. I could do this. Everyone else I knew had paved their own way. I was confident it would be an easy ride into parenthood. Yet if I really thought about it, despite the conscious decision to have a baby, there is a spark of nature that must comply. All the mystical elements of conception must be timed correctly in order to change the lines on the pregnancy test.

My husband and I took for granted the ease at which I got pregnant. During pregnancy, I noted the lack of mood swings, nausea, and bloating. I hardly felt any different for months on end, and the barest little bump showed up in my sixth month of pregnancy. I wanted to feel different, to be cognizant of it all, to commiserate with all my friends who were newly pregnant too. But I felt stuck in limbo, feeling neither one way nor the other. I went to every appointment, gave copious amounts of blood for tests, passed my gestational diabetes test, and began our birthing classes. I continued my habit of walking an hour a day, sometimes clocking in four or five miles depending on my energy level. I joked with my doctor that the baby would probably come fast since my workout habits were so good. He smiled amicably but probably noticed my naivety and let it be, knowing that life was a toss of the dice. You can never determine how anyone's birth plans would go. I was confident, perhaps overconfident. From my perspective, all the pieces of the puzzle were falling into place. I was happily living out my own little fairy tale.

We were required to take an infant CPR class, which was held at the hospital. During a breakout session, we were taught how to practice CPR on a dummy. It was in that class we met another young couple. I couldn't help but notice the woman's belly was protruding. Given that we were in a CPR maternity class, I asked the obvious.

"When is your baby due?"

She glanced at her husband, then gave a slightly pained smile. "We had our baby last week. He's in the NICU."

My smile faded. "Oh, goodness. I'm sorry for asking. I just thought . . ." I trailed off, embarrassed and at a loss for words.

"It's okay," she said. "We never got a chance to take the class because he came six weeks early. So here we are. I guess we'll be prepared in case anything happens when we bring him home." She looked so young at that moment, like a frightened child glancing at her husband for reassurance.

"I'm sure everything will be fine," I reassured her, already feeling like a mom from my privileged perch at thirty-five weeks pregnant. After class, they picked up their coffee cups, eager to head out. As she slung her shiny new diaper bag over her shoulder, our eyes met and I smiled at her. They were headed back to the NICU to keep watch over their baby.

As Erik and I walked out of the hospital, I turned to him as if we were the insulated ones. "Thank God that won't be us," I whispered, blissfully unaware that we were about to enter the world of parenthood completely unprepared for the other side of perfect.

Chapter Three

The month I became pregnant with Owen was exactly as I had planned and anticipated. Erik and I booked a delayed honeymoon to Europe, which was tagged on to my business trip to Germany. We rented a car and drove from Munich through Austria and then south into Italy, stopping to visit a Venetian friend of mine, Tiziana, whom I hadn't seen in years. Erik was reluctant to visit Venice.

"I've been there before. It's dirty," he explained. But he didn't know the Venice I knew, when I spent summers with Tiziana in the depths of the city, wandering through narrow cobblestone streets, stopping for a coffee, or spending late nights at an after-hours "club" in someone's palatial home.

"You haven't seen the *real* Venice," I told him. "Wait until you see my Venice." We joined Tiziana's family for dinner where we were served classic Venetian dishes followed by a bottle of grappa the restaurant owner gifted our table that night. The next day, we explored Venice: the bakery down the street from her third-story, Venetian Gothic home; the cheese shop; and the fish market, making our way to San Marcos Square. We walked deep within the city, finding churches whose doors were open.

"You're right. The real Venice is beautiful," Erik admitted. Although our trip had started in Munich, we spent most of our time in Italy, driving through the countryside, exploring villages and cities.

Within two weeks of our return, I was staring at a positive pregnancy test. The timing was exactly as I had expected; my planning had been perfectly calculated. I now wondered how I could determine if I was having a boy or a girl based on my ovulation.

According to my calculations, I was five weeks pregnant as I stared at a barely-there line on a pregnancy test. I bit my lip as I sat in the bathroom, holding it first this way, then that way to see if the line appeared any darker. It was the faintest line, but as I had been told, a line is a line. In my ignorance, I assumed that the line was valid and I was pregnant. Sure enough, I was. Pregnant. Right? But I didn't feel a bit different, and I (wrongly) assumed that the minute I became pregnant, something must feel different in my body. Nothing did. I crossed each day off with a pencil on my desk calendar, feeling minutes tick by like mud slowly moving centimeter by centimeter over a slanted rock. My life was lived minute by minute. I was unprepared for the nothingness of it all in the early weeks. I made an appointment with my doctor for what would be a two-month checkup. There was no drama, no urgent sense of feeling sick, no cravings. I called my mom to ask her if my pregnancy experience was normal. She told me she couldn't remember if she was ever sick with any of us because so many times she was still breastfeeding when she got pregnant. To her credit, when you've had nine kids and been pregnant eleven times, it must somehow all fuse together. I called my sisters after my mom couldn't offer any specifics. How did they feel? What felt different? I peppered them with questions. When my decidedly unpregnant-like body wasn't cooperating, I took to journaling. Perhaps if I wrote about my bodily sensations and emotions, something would stick out as different. At our twelve-week ultrasound, Erik went with me to hear the heartbeat. My doctor told me that for eleven weeks, the baby looked good and was developing on schedule.

"Eleven weeks?" I questioned. By my endless calculations, the baby was assuredly twelve weeks along, since I knew exactly when we got pregnant and when I was ovulating.

"Nope, the baby is due July fourth, according to the ultrasound," he said matter-of-factly. I was perplexed. It couldn't be right. My calculations meant he should be born a week earlier. Respectfully, I let it slide since I wasn't the medical professional. My new due date was now the birthdate of the United States of America.

As soon as we got home from the doctor, Erik's mom, Eva, called. She wanted to know every detail. When I told her that the baby's due date was July 4, she instantly berated me for originally telling her the baby's due date was a week earlier.

"You've been telling me the due date for two months now! How could they change it like that?" she questioned. Her tone played on the assumption that I was somehow wrong.

"That's what they told me." I shrugged, though she couldn't see me. Eva always had the ability to make me feel she needed convincing. "But I swear my dates were correct."

"Well, you aren't a doctor, are you?" she said in an overbearing tone. Throughout the years I had been dating her son, an underlying friction had crept between us. Nothing I did was ever quite good enough. Frankly, I tried really hard to soothe any hostility she had toward me, but she found a way to turn the smallest details into a battleground. The cake at her son's birthday party was an issue because I bought it from the wrong bakery. A Christmas present I spent hours shopping for her was thrown aside with a sour look on her face. Even when I brought a dish for Christmas—one year it was my mom's famous German potato salad, which was a staple in my parents' house on Christmas day—she laughed and said it was food you serve at a barbecue on paper plates. I took to bringing only wine because I knew she couldn't compete with me on selecting a good bottle. I had been schooled in the variations of taste, bouquet, and regions much better than her from my days working in the events industry.

At our twenty-two-week ultrasound, they told us the heartbeat was strong. The following week, my doctor surveyed the test results and paused for a moment.

"How tall is your husband?" he asked.

"He's six foot seven," I responded, wondering where this line of questioning was going.

"Well, the thigh bone looks more like your size than your husband's," my doctor noted.

"Maybe that means it's a girl." I stated hopefully. But we had chosen not to find out the sex, and the doctor didn't confirm or deny my statement.

Months earlier, my doctor and I had the conversation about prenatal testing, specifically CVS (chorionic villus sampling) testing. I asked him if he thought I should.

"What would you do if you found out your baby had a chromosomal disorder?" he asked, his eyes holding mine.

"I don't want to be faced with a decision," I said, arrogantly assuming there would be no issues.

"Then, my dear, you have already decided not to take the test," the doctor replied with a smile. I appreciated his answer because I absolutely believed that if there was anything I could do well, it was to birth a perfect baby. *No need for testing here*, I thought to myself comfortingly.

A year prior, Eva had affirmed my confidence in birthing the "perfect child." One casual afternoon at our house in Hollywood, I invited her in for a glass of wine after a day of shopping. The day had ended with a beautiful sunset that quietly dropped over the Hollywood Hills. Erik and I had only been married a few months, but the glow of the wedding and festivities hadn't yet faded.

"I suppose you two will have kids," Eva said.

"I think we'll wait a year to try," I responded.

"Well, you can't wait forever. You've already waited too long to get married." I laughed off-handedly. "They give all these fancy tests nowadays. Are you going to take them when you do become pregnant?" Her question was innocent enough, but I knew she had a valid point tucked in there.

With great assurance, I said, "I don't think I have anything to worry about. Not the way my mother breeds."

She nodded. "Yep, you sure proved that your family has brought more than enough kids into the world."

My confidence was high, and my thoughts were drunk on the possibilities of the life we would live, despite the barbed comments Eva casually flung at me.

Chapter Four

Owen was born two weeks early on a summer day that registered 115 degrees Fahrenheit in my car. The day before, as a public relations executive, I had crammed in as much as I could: a breakfast meeting followed by a full day at the office, capped off by a board meeting. I arrived home around ten o'clock that night, exhausted, my feet aching as I reached unsteadily around my belly to take off my heels. The silk lilac shirt I wore most days had a spot on it, which I hadn't noticed until now. It was the only shirt in my ninth month of pregnancy that fit my huge belly and hung down long enough that my legs actually appeared slim—though nothing truly appears slim when you are nine months pregnant. That night, I slept more soundly than I had in weeks, the ache in my wrists from pregnancy-induced carpal tunnel syndrome had dissipated. Most nights I wore wrist braces, each filled with a tiny ice pack to stem the piercing pain that always woke me up.

The next morning, after I got out of the shower and toweled off, I began to dress and felt water dribbling down my leg. I had an inkling something was different, but I refused to believe it. The big event was still two weeks away and, having never given birth before, I believed this baby would not dare show its face before I had completed every single task on my to-do list. Counting down the days, I jammed my calendar with as many meetings as I could manage until the birth.

Midmorning, I attended a website meeting, unable to concentrate because my nerves were rattled. I nibbled on a small nectarine but could barely eat. Strange, I was hugely pregnant at this point and wolfed anything down in sight, but the hunger was not present today. I excused myself and headed to the bathroom, again feeling liquid seeping down my leg. My body felt chilly as my hands became clammy. The words "not yet" echoed through my mind. I called my mom, who advised me to call my doctor right away. I patiently explained that I still had things to do. I wasn't quite ready for a complete life change—at least not today.

"Nobody ever is," she said, then reminded me with an increased tone of urgency to call my doctor. I felt like a child who didn't know what to do. A child who was waiting for instructions from an adult. Erik said the same thing when I called him, and I could sense the worry in his voice since the drive to my doctor's office was forty-five minutes away. I kept working, furiously answering emails as fast as I could, debating what to pack and take with me, unsure if I was coming back today, tomorrow, or . . . after the baby was born. As my thoughts were racing, a colleague stepped into my office, her arms crossed.

"Go home," she said. I looked up, wondering how she knew.

"Your husband just called the front desk and told me your water broke. Get out of here; otherwise, we'll have to call you an ambulance because none of us has ever delivered a baby."

I froze, then nodded, haphazardly picking up files and papers and stuffing them into my briefcase. I looked around one last time and left, oddly aware my colleagues were watching me as I walked out of the building. I had no idea I was in active labor, but it was happening. I drove to my doctor's office, where women lined the chairs in the small waiting room in various stages of pregnancy. Dr. Pearson's nurse ushered me in right away, and I felt a twinge of guilt, recalling the times I sat in those chairs, bored with the magazines that littered the tables, waiting longer than I thought necessary because a woman had come in with an emergency.

My doctor seemed puzzled. "Your water hasn't broken. It's just leaking. That means we'll have to get the baby out sooner rather than later. Get your things and head over to the hospital. I'll meet you there."

I looked at him wide-eyed. "I can't. I have a meeting this afternoon," I said, convinced I was still going to carry on with my preplanned tasks. My baby was not due for two more weeks. I was *not* ready to be a mom today. I didn't realize until that very moment the terror I harbored knowing I was going to have a child. I was faced with the monumental undertaking of absolute surrender to what was going to happen that was not previously worked out on a white board. My hands started shaking.

Dr. Pearson put his hand on my shoulder and looked me in the eye. "My dear, you are going to have a baby. As luck would have it, you will have time to cancel your meeting." He chuckled, and I wondered if I sounded crazy to him. I felt sick to my stomach, not sure if it was from excitement or the fact that the only food in my stomach was the lone nectarine I ate for breakfast. Erik looked at me in happy surprise when I came into the waiting room.

"Let's go have a baby," I said, my throat dry. The waiting room was small, and the women who heard me turned to look, then offered smiles and words of encouragement that followed me out like a warm hug. I wasn't prepared. I didn't have a manual for the unexpected. All I knew was that I was going to have this baby. Today.

Chapter Five

Once in the hospital, I lay in bed, writhing from contractions. I was not prepared for this level of pain. It was indescribable; words fail to convey the all-consuming radius of physical agony. I was now fully immersed in childbirth, and I desperately wanted out. The epidural softened the pain, but the nurses paged the doctor because they could tell the baby was in distress. When Dr. Pearson arrived, he listened to the heartbeat.

"Are you still on board with that C-section?" he asked.

I nodded, fully medicated but still in pain. We had discussed a C-section prior to this, and I had secretly hoped for one so I didn't have to go through the pain. As I was to learn, C-sections create their own kind of pain.

The nurses wheeled me into a surgical room and prepped me, and from what seemed like far away I heard a beep, flatlining loud and clear. I couldn't be sure whose monitor it was since my body lay prone, lethargic and heavy. In my drugged state, I knew I was still breathing, barely registering I was listening to my baby's heartbeat. The doctor was paged immediately, and within minutes he made the cut into my abdomen. Seconds passed, and I felt a tugging within my body as he skillfully extracted my baby.

"It's a boy!" I heard a weak cry, and the nurses swaddled him and brought him into my line of vision. I was bone tired but aware enough to notice a clump of dark-red hair. As they brought him to the scale, I saw the back of him. Then I noticed his flattened head, curved spine, tiny arms, and legs that were still curled up as if he wasn't aware he was out of my womb. Suddenly, an image of a tiny broken bird flashed through my mind. I filed that thought as a hallucinatory byproduct from all the medication.

His APGAR score was high, and Erik hugged his aunt Elly, who had scrubbed in for surgery. As a retired nurse with Providence St. Joseph Hospital—otherwise known as St. Joe's—she often sent delicious carrot cakes to the staff when she had a friend or family member in labor and delivery, a gentle coaxing for them to pay special attention to the patient.

"A healthy baby boy," she said, her smile wide and her expansive girth still encased in green scrubs. Who knew those words would be so right yet so wrong? He was healthy. He was strong. He was alive and here. But the next few weeks would reveal another layer to the story.

As I lay sleeping off the drugs, Erik followed the baby to the nursery where his breathing prompted the nurse to put an oxygen mask on him. My son, who was less than one hour old, pulled the mask off his face as the nurses tried to position it again.

"If that isn't a strong baby, I don't know what is," Erik told me later, and his smile declared that he was already in love. The nurses suspected fluid in the baby's lungs from the C-section and whisked him off to the NICU. Meanwhile, I was shuttled upstairs to a private room to recover. As nurses came in to check my vitals, they also wheeled in a free-standing machine with tubes hanging down. In my fuzzy state of mind, I had no idea what it was until a nurse casually mentioned it was a breast pump. I didn't understand, and honestly, because of the C-section incision, I didn't want to get out of bed. The nurses came in at intervals to help me get to the bathroom. My mind was depleted. I didn't know what I was supposed to do other than sleep. My baby had been born at 7:30 p.m., and I vaguely recall a phone conversation with my mom, communicating that I'd delivered a boy. I had never known such tiredness, and since this was my first time ever having surgery, I was completely in the dark about what recovery looked like. I don't remember much from the first night except random interruptions by nurses to check on me.

The next day dawned, and I called the nurse to ask when I could see my son. She explained he was in the NICU and I would have to go see him, not the other way around. Immediately, my mind jumped to a task list. I had to get better. I had to get out of bed. I had to get dressed. I had to do something with that pump. Phones calls came in during the day, but because my baby was in the NICU, I had no visitors except for Erik. It was a little unsettling being in surgery, then sleeping in the room overnight by myself with nothing reminding me of home except the bag I packed, sitting on the chair. I hadn't anticipated such a sterile room and so many hours by myself. I was so disconnected to the moment, to my baby, to everything.

Without a baby to hold, I wasn't even sure I was a mother yet. We walked slowly down the hall to the elevator, mindful of my incision and the surgery. I was trying to rectify the energetic person I had been the day before to a body that was now bruised, cut, and slowly trundling down the hall, pain with every step. A feeling of frustration at my limitations overcame me. I had never anticipated surgery, and because of that, I was blindsided with the suddenness of it all, the intensity of the pain, and the blood. All the blood.

The little guy was in an incubator when I visited him for the first time, tied to an oxygen machine and a heart monitor. Wires ran all over him like spider webs with multiple colors that traversed his body. He had a cut under his eye where the scalpel had nicked him, and his tiny foot was blue from the blood they had drawn. It wasn't until later I found out he was situated in my stomach in a "brow presentation," so his face was smashed right up against my stomach, neck arched. Because of the position and the immediacy in which they had to get him out, when my doctor cut into my abdomen with his scalpel, he was unaware my baby's tiny face was pushed up right where the incision needed to be made, missing his eye by only a few centimeters.

I gazed at him, marveling at his tiny body, fingers, and toes. I was having a hard time processing that he was my child. This wasn't the way I'd imagined it. I thought that rainbows would follow me and the world would be colored in pastels. Instead, we watched our baby flail about in a plastic box connected to tubes and monitors. I held him; the newness of his tiny body so delicate in my arms. A part of me felt so unprepared, and perhaps two more weeks would have given me a bit more time. But the results would have been the same. We named him Owen, a Welsh name that meant *wellborn.* It also meant *young warrior,* which seemed fitting given his entry into the world, and the glint of red hair exposed the Irish roots of my family's side.

Three days passed while I recovered in the hospital. I didn't know what to tell anyone. There were no answers given to us, and I was busy trying to get myself back to where I was, as if the surgery was something I could bounce back from right away. When people called to ask about the baby, I gave vague answers. Our visitors were few, and I wanted desperately to feel like things would be back to normal soon.

I went home on the third day, Erik and I arriving at the house feeling oddly unsure how to play this parenting game when we didn't have a baby with us. The house felt chilly and hollow, despite the heat of the day. The baby's crib sat in the corner, along with unopened baby items, tiny outfits printed with baby giraffes, pacifiers, and plush blankets from the shower I'd recently had. Recovering from surgery meant my days consisted of bed rest and going to see our son in the hospital. During the hours in between, I fielded more phone calls but noticed myself retreating as people asked what was going on with Owen. I didn't know, and I didn't know what to ask the doctors or how to start the process of understanding what was normal and what wasn't. I began to avoid the calls from family and friends, hoping we would get an answer soon.

The NICU was a soothing, gentle place with hushed voices and soft blankets that had been made for the babies. An unknown woman had stitched together a quilt that lay over my son, decorated with puppy dog toes and rainbows. I loved it immediately and imagined the day I would remind Owen of these few precious days that were the start to his life. My big, strong boy and I would reminisce about this blip in his life, a momentary glitch in the birth story I had imagined.

Monitors beeped everywhere while babies of all sizes slept in tiny incubators. There is something conspiratorial by nature when you have a child in the NICU. The nurses smiled, and laughed, and welcomed us. They told us his stats every time we came in, their cheeriness and warm smiles intending to put us at ease. Perhaps it was their way of disarming the victim before they deliver the bad news. I began breastfeeding as soon as I could, despite the comments that I didn't have to if it would be too difficult with the oxygen and monitor wires. The first few times I tried, hovering nurses made it difficult for me—and Owen—as they instructed and watched. I persevered, and when he latched on, my body relaxed, and I felt victorious in a way that only new moms can. I proved to myself that when the stakes were high, I could enter warrior-mode, bestowing a liquid serum that would heal my baby's body faster.

The days unfolded, and by the sixth day we were tired of questions from family about when Owen would come home. The NICU staff brushed us off with the same rote lines that he was "progressing well with his oxygen." The cut under his eye was healing, lessening the look of a baby boxer who'd taken a left hook to the eye. We hadn't met our pediatrician yet because Owen was in the NICU, and my doctor was busy helping the next group of women birth their babies. I felt untethered, suspended in a universe where I didn't have any answers to help me make any decisions or to help me plan the next steps.

"Tomorrow we should have answers," the nurse said brightly as she continued to busy herself with the babies.

Interestingly, whenever we pass St. Joe's and I remind my son he was born there, he expounds on how that hospital is his "hometown," since he truly believes he began his childhood there. He rattles off the year and day he was born, then asks me questions about who was there, where he slept, and what he ate. He asks me to recreate his beginning, and sometimes I indulge him. Maybe he's not far off. Maybe all of us, in our own way, need to identify our beginning, our "hometown," to have a place, a definition, of how our story unfolds. After all, St. Joe's is the place that our stories merged—Owen's story, Erik's story, and my story—where the people we were before we arrived are no more. We were first one, then we became two, and then we became three. The door we walked through on that day in July was like our own *Alice in Wonderland*, falling down the hole into a world that didn't make sense at first. We arrived at a place that was simultaneously magical and dark, bitter and sweet, odd and wonderful. But we survived the fall, and that's what counts.

Chapter Six

It was July 3, one day before our nation's celebration of independence, and a palpable excitement hummed between Erik and me as we drove to the hospital. Today was the day we could bring our baby boy home. As we entered the NICU, I noticed his isolette had been moved to the farthest corner.

"He's over there," a nurse said, indicating Owen's location with a smile and nod. Her NICU-nurse softness was something I had learned to lean into.

"Maybe they do that when the baby's ready to go home," I mentioned to Erik.

Holding him, I looked around and realized we had been placed next to a security door that banged every time it shut, startling Owen. His tiny hands flinched and his eyes enlarged, the harsh noise unfamiliar and unwelcome to his fragile body. The lights seemed brighter, flat and colorless, and his new placement removed him from the hub of activity.

A doctor I had never met strode over to us, her dark, fuzzy hair framing her face like a halo, her heels creating a staccato tap on the floor as she approached. She was speaking to us in words that were hard to understand—English not being her first language. My brain was desperately trying to decode what she was saying. I heard the words *Down syndrome*, but they couldn't be meant to describe Owen. For a split second, I felt bad for the couple whose news it was, because it certainly wasn't our baby's diagnosis. She continued speaking, and as the fog in my head cleared a bit, I strung her words into a sentence.

"The test came back positive today. He has Down syndrome."

I shook my head to signal no. We were not waiting for any tests. I smiled slightly.

"You must have the wrong family. We are waiting to be discharged," I said, politely pointing out her error.

She looked again at the paperwork and glanced at the monitor where his name was taped.

"Baby Lezotte. It's confirmed. Diagnosis of Down syndrome." She paused for a moment, and I stood there motionless. "Were you not aware of the test?" Her eyes caught mine, and she stood there with no emotion, file in hand, holding a piece of paper that had just turned my world upside down. We had never met, and now this woman would be indelibly marked on my brain as a turning point to a new direction. Couldn't she see that we were happy? We merely needed the paperwork to release our child so we could walk out into the bright sunshine and start our new family of three. I didn't anticipate this stranger was going to drop the words Trisomy 21—the clinical term for Down syndrome—on us like a science test we hadn't studied for.

I felt a chill sweep over me as the hairs on my arms bristled, though the sun shone brightly into the room on that summer day. Machines beeped in intervals, the only noise as a thick silence settled between us. A random burst of laughter came from a nurse on the other side of the room before my hearing shut down and all the noises became a drone in my head. Physically, Owen was healthy, but his internal chromosome combination was one of the most common survivable genetic anomalies in humans. In the week prior, we were blissfully unaware.

I felt nauseous, looking at my baby who had suddenly become a diagnosis, a chromosomal abnormality, a statistic. I was too. I now had a label. I instantly became part of a group of people who would forever lay claim to the statistics of science. My husband stood up to find the restroom, walking unsteadily across the floor.

"I think I'm going to pass out," he said, and someone triggered the alarm for assistance. Within minutes, nurses surrounded him, helping him to a chair and handing him juice.

It was my baby's eyes, the way they held their gaze on mine as if he knew. They were calm, a murky dark gray blending into blue. If I looked closely, I could see tiny shards of crystal in his eyes. I would come to learn they were called iris brush spots. They added an aura and depth to his eyes as he watched me while the news seeped into my brain. He looked at me as if he knew what my thoughts were at this moment: the bad thoughts, the evil thoughts. For one long, dripping moment, I thought that maybe it would have been better if he had died. In that moment, like quicksand, I wanted to be swallowed whole, to disappear from this fateful moment. This delivery of news that had never crossed my mind. I held this brand-new human in my arms as tears began to sprout from my eyes and splash onto his alabaster arms. His tiny baby bones were so fragile, so new. Owen's fate was also my fate to own.

My hands shook as I handed the baby back to the nurse. I thought of the C-section and the flatlining, then the ghastly thought floated through my mind again.

Maybe it would have been better if he had died. I tried to erase the dark thoughts as soon as they came, but they floated like a black mist. Knowing who Owen is now and embracing the life he led us to, I shudder to recall those fear-based, reactive thoughts. But it was the most honest, raw assessment my mind could conceive. I had only known him for seven days, and the experience up until then had been major surgery, a breastfeeding machine, and a tiny baby tethered to machines. I was experiencing a mixture of feelings that ranged from confusion, to anger, to sadness. Now I understood why they transferred him to the back of the room. Who wants crazy parents crying and fainting? I'm sure they didn't anticipate a scene, but I was aware of the nurses looking at us furtively, trying not to stare. If I'm honest, I could swear I read pity on their faces.

Within the hour, a woman joined our huddle as we grasped

what had been told to us. My thoughts ping-ponged in my brain, restless and seeking. She was young, barely a step out of college, her demeanor solemn. She introduced herself as the hospital's social worker and handed me a pack of papers. She looked appropriately subdued, as if she worked at a funeral parlor.

"I understand what you are going through," she said as I stared straight at her. My eyes widened as I almost blurted, "Bullshit, bitch! You have no idea." She hardly looked old enough to have children, let alone coach me on what I was going through. I continued to stare her down, but this time with a bit of contempt.

"The papers contain information for services for his diagnosis, including support groups." She paused. No response from me must have made her feel that her job was done, so she left. I wanted to cry and scream, but more than anything I wanted to ask St. Joe's why they hadn't sent a nun, a good old-fashioned Catholic nun to comfort me instead of a barely-out-of-college social worker. She was a reminder to me at that moment of how unfair I felt this world was. She still had her whole life to have kids, and here we were, our first child barely a week old, and we had been given a life-changing diagnosis I never thought would cross my path. We sat in shock, tears rolling down our faces.

Had I known the news we were about to receive, I would have prepared myself differently perhaps. Maybe I would have cried before we arrived, or maybe I would have jumped straight into planning and researching—anything to change the numbness that settled on me in those first few moments of knowledge. During those first six days in the NICU, there was no hint to a different outcome. We were ignorant of the battery of tests they ran that would change the course of our lives. We had assumed that any day now they would release Owen, then we would come home and our joyous parenthood journey would begin. We were ready for the ecstasy of the event, the pink and blue balloons, the flowers, the smiles of sheer joy amid what we knew were more practical details: lack of sleep, an infant's cries, and dirty diapers. What we weren't expecting was the news we faced that day.

Chapter Seven

I have to compose myself so Owen will never know how I felt, I thought, wiping away tears as fast as they rolled down my cheeks. I summoned the strength to stop crying. I was good at covering up my emotions and forging ahead. I spent years masking my fears, running away. I could pretend I was managing. There would be days ahead that I could pull the covers over my head and retreat. But not now. Not today. Today was about putting one foot in front of the other, sweeping the feelings away, and surviving.

I looked at my son, my sweet Owen, lying there with his hands flailing. I decided that no matter what, he needed us; we were going to be his mirror into the world. We could either show him an amazing place with great potential, or we could weep and grieve and feel hopeless. At that moment, my newfound mother instinct took over, and like a lion who would fight for her cub's life, I knew that I would fight for Owen to have what he deserved: a good, loving support system and the freedom to explore the world in any way he chose. I wiped my tears and smiled at him, suited myself into imaginary armor, and began the process of healing.

Erik and I left the hospital to get lunch on the advice of the staff, who told us it would take time to process his paperwork given the new information of his diagnosis. When the doors opened to the fresh air outside, I inhaled deeply. Despite a half-hearted attempt at eating, we both knew we needed to go back, to face the new reality that had been thrust upon us. I rolled the days back in my mind: Had I known something was wrong? Had I suspected?

The moment we found out would haunt me for years. How my world darkened briefly, as if someone had died, taking with them the color of my surroundings. I can still picture the gray hospital walls, the black machines that monitored Owen's heartbeat, and the sterile handle that led to the corridor. Only yesterday, I saw the warm colors of the blankets that snuggled the tiny babies, the fresh pink and blue hues of the nurses' pajama-like outfits, and the smiles they bestowed on parents as they busied themselves with tiny humans. On this day, I felt Owen had been given an unfair start, a disadvantage, one that he would live with for the rest of his life. Unlike other diagnoses, this was permanent, a stamp on his genetic code. All these thoughts, I would eventually understand, were perfectly normal—and necessary for grieving. I was about to embark on a new journey most parents never take. Like life, you either step up and meet it head on, or you pull out of the game. I recalled reading a quote that said, "Grace always bats last." I chose to play ball and found a love like I have never known.

Until then, I had never been faced with such an overwhelming moment in my life. In one instant, Erik and I went from believing our son had a few minor problems to hearing a life sentence underscore our world. Down syndrome . . . the words even sounded depressing. I foolishly felt that I could tempt fate. I was blithely unafraid of it happening to me because all indicators from our families showed no anomalies. In fact, because my family had procreated so well and with such healthy results, I honestly believed there was no way anything like this could touch my genetic code. It came to my mind that I was flawed; I had failed Erik and failed my son by bringing him into this world. I started thinking of the what-ifs which pivoted to "Why me?" Thoughts pinged and circled and collided in my mind. We both sat there, no words forthcoming. I couldn't even look Erik in the eye. I didn't know what to say. I couldn't have formed a coherent thought if I tried. I kept thinking that if you had a child with Down syndrome, don't they look a certain way and act a certain way? Our son looked like any other newborn.

I thought back to the day before I went into labor. I hadn't slept well. We had run out of coffee, and I was late for work. My kitten kept tugging at my purse, and I couldn't understand why, until I got closer. Inside my purse was a dead baby bird, and she was trying to retrieve it. I recoiled and immediately called Erik to put it outside. With my stomach churning, I left the house, the image stuck in my brain. Driving down the hill, I came upon a green light and proceeded to cross the intersection, only to see a Suburban careening toward me, tempting fate as the woman driver sped through the beginning of her red light. Our eyes connected for a moment, and I gunned my car through the intersection. She swerved. What would my life had been like had she hit me that day? What could have happened to my baby? I prayed during my whole pregnancy for a baby who was healthy, and Owen was born healthy. Most importantly, he was alive. My prayers were answered.

Months later, my doctor told me he was a lucky guy to be alive; had I progressed to pushing, he likely would have broken his neck because of his positioning. Flatlining, scalpel cut near miss, fetal positioning. There were so many instances where the outcome could have been different. All these puzzle pieces only added to my theory that grew from a tiny thought bubble and expanded. I rested in the knowledge that Owen was meant to be here, to change our lives, to teach us. Despite the barriers, he made it out alive and kicking. In fact, he never stopped moving from the day he was born. A nurse was stationed at his unit to make sure he didn't upset the oxygen tent with his constantly flailing arms and legs. Again, the image of a caged, broken bird came to me, almost like a spirit who needed to be set free.

That day defined me in a way no other could have. For the rest of my life, I would move toward the person I was destined to become precisely because of Owen's diagnosis. I would meet people who I would otherwise never have met. I was forced to recalibrate my life, my dreams, my spirituality, and the significance in which I saw my role as a mother. I had to choose, incrementally, as I walked this new path, what I would carry with me and what I needed to let go of. Until that day, I was fiercely loyal to the control that I exacted on my dreams and my beliefs. Control was what centered me; it righted my world when things were askew. Control was what I had left when everything around me had burned down. But I couldn't continue to live my life holding on to my old ideals. I couldn't figure out how to carry forward the old me without introducing bits and pieces of a new me, a reformed me, a person who now knew that vulnerability was part and parcel of life, and no amount of control could force it back into the box. I would have to succumb to nature, to peel back the layers of control, and to admit this path that opened up to me was my resurrection, my bridge to a new future.

Chapter Eight

We returned home again, childless, since the NICU staff advised Owen stay one more day to process all his stats. My mind was overloaded with an anxiety I hadn't known before; the next step was telling our families. For a few hours, we both tried to process the information without any outside influence. We lay down together in bed, where weeks before I had dreamed of our little one lying with us. Side by side, our hands tucked inside one another's as we both stared at the ceiling. No words came. Each of us remained locked in our own silent battle of thought. I wanted to shut my brain off, to delete what I knew, but I couldn't. The words *Down syndrome* infiltrated every thought I had. After what felt like an infinite amount of time, I sat up. I needed to shower. Lying down made my head hurt, warring with the beating of my panicked heart—not to mention, my surgical wound ached. I sat up carefully. My movement was limited and painful, yet the physical pain was nothing compared to the pain that had settled upon my heart.

With my back to Erik, I spoke. "Who do we tell first?" His silence followed me as I hoisted myself off the bed.

"I think we tell your parents first," I answered before he could speak. "Let's get the hardest part over with." We both knew his mom, Eva, would be the most judgmental and the most likely to shame us. We had a secret ally in his aunt and decided it would be wise to call her first to practice how we delivered the bad news. Even though I cringed at the thought of telling my parents, I knew that the faith they practiced all their lives as Catholics would hold them steadfast in their beliefs, and they would offer acceptance.

I went into the bathroom to shower, and all I could see was my body still swollen from the pregnancy, yet my stomach was deflated. My mind felt deflated, too, as if the balloon of wonder had popped. I felt as mushy and out of sorts as my body looked. Nobody had told me that this is how it would be, that the miracle of birth would have a lasting effect on the way you perceived yourself. I saw a mess, a big mess that needed to be cleaned up—both my newborn's diagnosis and myself. Erik came into the bathroom and we glanced at each other. While I looked at my flawed, fleshy body, he looked into the mirror at his own image. Dealing with his own internal voices, his eyes locked on mine.

"I came up with the only words I know that will help me get through this," Erik said. Then he paused, and I could tell by the shakiness in his voice that he was close to tears. "Dig deep," he continued in a low voice.

Looking at him, I saw a vulnerability etched on his face that I had never seen before. We were carving new emotions into our physical planes, our faces a pliable clay that was now being molded by invisible hands. We were reduced to children ourselves at this moment, unsure of how to play the hand we were dealt in a game that was new to us. To add more fear into the equation, our tiny newborn's life was at stake, whom we were tasked with nurturing and shaping into a loving, resilient, purpose-filled human. In the stillness of that moment, as we stood in our bathroom, the only sound I heard was the drip of the shower paired with the heat of the day seeping in through the window, and it made my throat ache. I wanted to cry and scream, to break the silence in any way I could. But I didn't. Those two words hovered in the air. I knew "dig deep" was what Erik needed—a phrase, a constant anchor that would rotate in his mind and keep him sane while we navigated our new world.

Neither of us wanted to tell Eva, but we knew she had to be first. Her standards were impeccably high, and I knew she would lay the blame at my feet. No subject was off-limits to her, and we sparred on almost everything. She asked me questions in a sunny, lilting voice and tore my answer apart until I was left wondering why I was on trial. It could be something as simple as the weather, and my answer became a battleground. Friends often told me to push back, but she caught me off guard so often that I had no response. Perhaps she should have been a lawyer—specifically a trial lawyer. She was deceptive in her line of questioning, luring me to take the bait and then reeling me in as she dissected my beliefs.

She was raised in Norway, a land of long summer days with even longer dark winter nights. When I first met her, I was captivated by the way she spent so much time on presentation. Her dinner table was a work of art, the intricate patterns of dinnerware, silverware, candles, and flowers carefully orchestrated. No matter how small the occasion, even if it was just the two of us dropping by for a glass of wine and appetizers, she never failed to produce elegant plates, napkins, silverware, and a centerpiece. Every holiday was an opportunity for her to set the table and invite family and friends over to remark on the spectacular display. Eva and I were at odds with the way I was raised. She considered my too-large family a stark contrast to her modestly sized family. She looked down on my upbringing, which was bolstered by her retelling my personal history of mismatched dinnerware, paper napkins, and paper plates that were always at the ready for impromptu pizza nights. Her look of disgust was apparent the first time I suggested paper plates for an outdoor party in Malibu.

"Not in my house," she'd said with disgust, then went out and bought another set of glass plates, thereby circumventing the need for any more talk of paper products. She often stopped by with platters and dishes for my table, then advanced to buying me clothing that she had me try on, insisting I stop what I was doing and try it on that moment. When it didn't fit, she would sigh heavily.

"If you lose those extra pounds, I bet it would fit and you

would look fabulous." Sometimes I wondered who she was shopping for: me or her?

When I tried to decorate my house for Christmas, she told me I didn't have any taste. The next day she stopped by with new decorations she "happened" to see in the store that would be perfect for my house. Slowly, my house turned into her house, and she would promptly show up as soon as it was early enough to put up decorations, transforming my house while I was at work. I was an ancillary part of her plan to set her mark on my life. Perhaps I was her do-over. A chance for her to dress me, school me, and set me back in a house she approved of. Her very own living doll.

Erik and I finally pulled ourselves together enough to leave the house so we could get the family talks over as soon as possible. Owen would be released the next day, but without the opportunity to clear the air, to make everyone aware that we would be bringing our child home with nothing else weighing on our mind but his growth, we needed those conversations to happen this afternoon, to be followed by an evening call with my parents.

Murmuring his mantra, Erik dialed his aunt's number and as fast as he could told her the situation. Her disbelief was apparent, as we had all been caught unaware of the situation. She immediately asked, "How are you going to tell Eva?" Everyone on some level feared Eva's reaction.

Erik asked his aunt if she could meet us at his parents' house to help deliver the news. She agreed. By the time we arrived, she had beat us there, and the look on Eva's face told us she already knew. A tiny piece of me was relieved I didn't have to tell her, as I could see that to her it was like receiving notice of a family member's death. I silently agreed with her. The son I thought I was going to have had died. But a little tiny newborn was alive, and that is who I was going to fight for.

We sat in the kitchen, the five of us, the air thick with thoughts unspoken. Erik's dad, a man of few words, said nothing, yet I felt his unwavering support. So many nights we had spent in that kitchen celebrating, playing cards, or having conversations. But today, the pall of a waning summer day cast a shadow over us all. The random scent of jasmine wafted in, and for a moment I felt as if I couldn't breathe. It was surreal, as if I had stepped into someone else's life and was watching everyone sit there, frozen, a tableau of a family coming to terms with spoken words that just didn't match the day.

Eva finally spoke. "We all know I would have chosen differently, but here we are, and here he is." The elephant in the room had been placed defiantly and precisely in the midst of us all, and she had the nerve to name it.

I never considered that Erik or I might have bucked the system; that all those odds had come to a point where the wheel of fortune chose someone. It was our turn to be here now, in her kitchen, the domain where she raised two typical boys. We came with the sobering news that our child was born with a disability. Once you release those words, you can't take them back; they forever mar the joy of a baby's birth and define the next steps in all of your relationships.

The day lengthened, and Eva got up.

"I suppose I'll put something out to eat. You must be hungry," she said. And in her Scandinavian manner, she rustled up some food for everyone and fetched beer for Erik and his dad. As empty as my cup felt at that moment, a bit of life had trickled back into it. The worst of the telling was over. We now had to call my parents. Eva offered her phone upstairs so we could have privacy, since it was getting late, and my parents were on East Coast time. Erik and I went up to their room, and my hands shook as I dialed the phone.

My dad picked up, happy to hear from me. When I asked him to get Mom on the phone, I could hear a bit of panic in his voice. She came on the line and I willed myself not to cry just yet. I had to get it out.

"Mom, Dad, our baby has Down syndrome," I said, choking on the last part. My Dad went silent, and I knew he didn't trust himself to talk. Mom did what she had done all our lives when we fell into a crisis: she talked. She talked about what a blessing he was and how God had chosen us to be his parents. She went on about how the universe was never wrong. She talked as Erik and I hung on her words like two people lapping up drops of water in the desert. I don't know how she knew what to say, she just did. Was it because she had shepherded nine children into adulthood? Her wisdom was so necessary and so heartfelt, and we both sobbed as she spoke.

"You are both going to be okay, and so is Owen." I drank those words in.

"Thanks, Mom," I whispered. As we said our goodbyes, my dad could barely get out any words.

"I love you, Sue," he said, my childhood nickname instinctively surrounding me with nostalgia for a childhood long gone. As I hung up, I felt more tears roll down my cheeks.

Telling the rest of my family was, in a way, like bowling; as soon as I told one person, it would be retold to the next one, and on to the cousins, aunts, and uncles, then I would have a strike. The news in my family—good or bad—always spread like wildfire. I could count on that for sure. A few people were missed along the way, siblings who I wasn't in contact with as frequently, or who had much more going on to pay attention. A few days later, my sister Marie called me.

"Mom and Dad told me you had some news about the baby," she said hesitantly.

"They didn't tell you?" I asked, trying to judge if she already knew and wanted to confirm it from me, or if she was completely in the dark.

"He didn't die, did he?" she whispered, fear lacing her voice.

I was thrown off guard for a second. "No, he has Down syndrome."

"Oh. Is that all?" Relief flooded her voice. "I thought it was worse. I had two beers before I could drum up the nerve to call you."

I thought it was worse. She was right. It could have been worse. We could have left the hospital without a baby, without any hope at all. But we had a baby, alive and kicking, who we had the opportunity to help shape and mold and love.

When Owen was born, I felt like I had been handed a different game to play and that my cards were labeled differently. It would take years before I realized that we all play our own game anyway

—despite what we think our kids will do based on what we encourage them to be. They make their own way in life, just as Erik and I had, and just as our parents had. Calling on my competitive nature that was honed in my childhood, I set my sights on a new scale. I was gunning for Owen to be the best kid in his league in whatever world that opened up to us as we started our journey. He would be my show pony, my trophy, in whatever competitive circle we chose to devise for him.

Chapter Nine

It still stung when I listened to a friend with a typical baby who had reached a milestone before Owen, or when a mom proudly announced that her baby's biggest hurdle had been cutting a new tooth. Everyone's baby seemed to be happy and wonderful and perfect. So each time I heard a new "amazing" story, it felt as if a barbed arrow had been shot into my heart. I made assumptions that probably weren't true. I imagined slights from family members, digs from fellow moms, or sideways looks from strangers. To counteract my paranoia, I tried to create my own fantasy. If I could keep Owen on track with typical babies, then maybe, just maybe, I could prove the scientific data wrong and this nightmare I was walking through would dissipate. But was it really that bad? I had a beautiful little baby who was trying as hard as any other. He was smiling, laughing, cooing, and teaching me to love him for exactly who he was. In my quest to weave this new story of a diagnosis into my life, I was overlooking the beautiful bits and pieces of his arrival into my life.

From the start, my family arrived in groups, knowing how physical comfort trumped any other kind of bond. My parents arrived when Owen was a month old, and to my dismay, I felt it was more of an intrusion than a welcome. Given that mentally I was in a dark place, I couldn't find the resources to act as if everything was okay when it wasn't, as if things hadn't changed, which they had. The hardest part with my parents was the thought that I had failed them.

As the daughter who got straight As, never asked for help, never got into trouble, and moved across the country in a carefully planned way, my new reality made me feel like everything I had done that was good was erased. In my mind, I couldn't do the easiest thing my family could do: procreate a perfect child. My dad was raised in a family of twelve kids, with two sets of twins. I couldn't even get one right.

But I watched as my dad held up brightly colored cards and tracked Owen's eye movements; something the in-hospital NICU staff had mentioned we should do right away to strengthen his eyes, since almost every person with Down syndrome has vision problems. My parents sat with him and moved his little arms and legs, hoping to build muscle coordination, just in case. This kid was doing more workouts by the time he was two months old than most kids do at that age. We were afraid his innate drive for movement wouldn't kick in like other kids; that he would be left behind.

A few months later, my sisters came to visit. I had spent too much time on the Internet, looking up stories of kids who died and moms who lost babies, as if I was looking for stories worse than mine so I could take a deep breath of relief. But those stories wormed their way into my brain—until one night when my sisters came at me with the hard truth. We were in Malibu, sitting outside on the deck, waves gently crashing in the background while Owen lay asleep inside. I uttered the words that I didn't think I could handle his diagnosis, especially if things got worse, and I felt weaker by my admission.

Marie spoke up. "You know, it's time you got over it. He's here. He has Down syndrome. Deal with it."

I didn't expect such harsh words. Nobody had been willing to speak so bluntly to me up until now, but it needed to be said. I needed someone to tell me to stop moping and get on with my role as a new mom.

My sister Celeste agreed. "Hey, nobody gets the perfect baby.

Remember Jackson and how he screamed for months with colic? Look at Owen. He's amazing and so cute. Just love him. Forget about what other people think or say."

"It's not that easy," I said, wiping away tears. "It's not easy to admit that I wish he hadn't been born with Down syndrome. And what if he gets early childhood leukemia? Or has a heart issue? Or worse yet, what if he dies?"

Marie spoke again. "You've had too many months to throw yourself a pity party. Enough!" I felt chastened, scolded. But she was right. It was time to let go of my fears. I had to deal with the here and now.

It was different with Erik's family. We were physically so much closer to them because we lived in the same city. His dad, Bob, embraced Owen from the moment he met him, diagnosis and all, just like Erik had.

Eva had a different opinion, and she reveled in making it known. As I stumbled along, learning to become a parent, she was right there, telling me what I was doing wrong, hardly ever complimenting me on doing anything right. Everything about Owen's birth was the exact opposite of how she had birthed her kids: from the pride in not gaining any weight, to barely having a cramp while birthing her son, to fitting into her jeans the next week—and nobody could ever compete with her experience. We used to joke behind her back that she must have farted and the baby came out effortlessly like a breeze. C-sections meant you were weak, she inferred, as if I had taken the "easy way out." I wondered why she had to be so boastful, so competitive with her son. Life was different now than it was in the days she raised her kids.

One Saturday, we headed to Malibu to spend the day with Erik's parents and his cousin, who'd recently had a baby girl. Eva had invited a few of her friends, and we all gathered around the outdoor table, drinking in the fresh Malibu air as the babies slept. The discussion gravitated, as it had ever since Owen was born, to whether we should have tested or not for Down syndrome. I felt as if I was always in fight mode, defending my position. I loved my little boy fiercely, and my job was to surround him with love, not doubt. Of course, Eva jumped in with her unfiltered opinion.

"Come on, Suzanne. If you had taken the test, you would have made a different decision." I was suffused with anger—again.

"Erik and I decided not to test because we weren't going to make a decision other than to have our baby," I shot back. She continued arguing with me, goading me on, trying to get me to admit that I would have chosen differently. The other women remained silent.

"Do you think I would have killed my son? He deserves a chance to live too." I told her I was done discussing it because we both had different ideas about the subject. Nobody chimed in to support me. It was as if Eva voiced the one opinion everyone was thinking but nobody would say to my face. I knew this because people casually seemed to ask me, "Did you take the test?" It was as if my world came down to that one question on a daily basis.

I looked at my son, who was sleeping peacefully in his car seat, and I felt sorry for him. I grieved the fact that so many people were already against him at the mere age of three months. I felt an immense sadness that even his grandmother didn't think he should have been given a chance. And I wondered if it was because Erik and I deliberately chose not to test that we were given a child with Down syndrome? That the universe knew we were willing to accept him, diagnosis and all?

Perhaps there was a hidden attribute that I was beginning to unearth inside me—a secret power that had lain dormant. I was about to embark on a battle to carve out an existence for my son in a world where not everybody saw him as worthy, or even equal for that matter. We had not questioned his right to life when he was just a tiny seed in my womb, so how did his diagnosis change that? No matter how "un-brave" I felt at the moment, I knew deep down there was a reserve in me that would rise up to become his greatest ally and his fiercest bodyguard with an ability to champion him against society's viewpoint, extra chromosome and all. I could tap into my greatest resource to accomplish this goal, my need to control my life, and now, by proxy, his life. But before I could tap into that, I had to walk through my own valley of sorrow and adjust my expectations. The road I started on involved coming to terms with the recognition that had I been given a choice. I would have sold my soul to take away his diagnosis. Yet what emerged was an appreciation for the world he was slowly unveiling to me: a world of inequality and discrimination. But also a world of champions, cheerleaders, and miracles.

Chapter Ten

My life had always been one big calendar. Everything was planned out, with start dates and end dates. I had a giant desk calendar so I could visualize everything when I sat down to work, as well as a small day planner tucked inside my purse. These were the days before iPhones became our default calendar, reminding us with a ping that it was time to be somewhere or do something. I was that person who looked forward to the end of the year when calendars were in stores everywhere. I poured over the new offerings, delighted with the opportunity to start over, to open the page to January 1. Nothing happened without my calendar, whether it was life goals that had dates in my mind, or big events that needed a timeline. When I was a senior in high school, I meticulously looked up the calendar for college, planning my trips to school, the holidays, and how long it would take me to graduate. Every summer I worked two jobs to pay for the next semester, then held a part-time job during school to offset expenses. By my fourth year, I was on target to graduate, never once taking out a student loan. My goals were clear-cut: graduate college and, degree in hand, move to a big city. When I decided on LA, I calendared it out. Work six months at a restaurant to save enough money to move, leave exactly on March 1, and in between those dates I would sort through what I needed, map out my journey, and start my new life.

To be suddenly thrown off course and have to adjust to nature's calendar was a jolt to my system. My baby had come two weeks early, throwing my first timeline into disarray, then he had stayed in the NICU for seven days, another discrepancy in my timeline. Finally, I was forced to confront head-on the warped timeline of a child with Down syndrome. In my new quest to take up the battle cry and become the warrior my son needed, I mulled over this wrinkle in my life.

The first person I met when I moved to LA was a colleague of mine at *Fortune* magazine. Cynthia appeared one night in the break room as I made a pot of coffee, only the janitors around to keep me company. I had been working on some writing after hours and took advantage of the quiet. She was surprised to find someone else willing to stay late and we quickly bonded, both of us single-minded in our determination to advance our careers. Working at a magazine where deadlines were crucial and always months ahead, we lived our lives in the future tense.

When I was given Owen's diagnosis of Down syndrome, I settled in with the information for a few days, only letting my family in on the news at first. One night, I felt compelled to call Cynthia, the weight of the diagnosis gnawing at me, and I couldn't shake the feeling that I wanted a piece of my old life back—a time when I was in complete control. It was late evening when I called her, and she was at dinner.

"Hey, Cyn, I have some news I need to tell you," I said. The din of the restaurant she was at made it hard for her to hear me.

"Zanne, hold on! Let me get to a quieter spot," she said, her nickname for me like a favorite jacket I slipped into. I nervously drummed my fingers on the kitchen counter. I could hear laughter and chatter in the background.

"I'm having dinner with a friend at the Beverly Wilshire. We have to come here some night!" she gushed. I was immediately transported to the days when we would find the best restaurant in town and, with our slim paychecks, order one appetizer and one glass of wine to be split between us. There was nothing I wanted more at that moment than to be transported back to those days. Tears silently slid down my face.

"Oh, Cyn, the baby has Down syndrome—" I blurted. I was still so raw that I couldn't even claim him as my own, he was "the" baby, not "my" baby.

"Hey, slow down. Take a breath," Cynthia interrupted before I could continue. She paused and then laughed, her exuberance in the face of what I thought was a tragedy put me at ease instantly. This was the reaction I expected from her and was one reason why I loved her. We had traveled so many adventures together, experienced so many situations in which we had learned to pivot, to turn the negative into a positive.

"Zanne, you got this. This is what we do, remember? When there's an issue, we break it down, work it out, plan it out. I'm not worried about you or the diagnosis. If there is anyone who can figure it out, it's you." Her words immediately rejuvenated me and filled me up. We all have that person in our lives who seems to be able to adjust a thought pattern, help us recalibrate. Cynthia was this person for me.

After that conversation, my mentality shifted a bit. I was used to a business plan: spell it out and work through the line items. I began to treat my son's life like a business plan. "These are the forms I have to fill out. This is the job I have to do. Here is how I will resolve these issues." Overwhelmed by the extra layer of work that surfaced, I called a few people we had been referred to for support. This was the beginning of my transition into an exclusive club that I had not applied for, but I was now a member, and it was time to get real and meet the rest of the group whom I would forever identify with. It was as if I had been holding my breath for the past few weeks since his birth. It was time to let out that giant expansion of air and relinquish the past. No going back.

Owen was an easy baby, and for the first few months of my maternity leave, he did everything any other baby did. He ate, slept, pooped, and even picked his head up and rolled over in a normal timeframe for milestones. From the first day home, we watched him like a hawk, reading books on baby milestones, checking to see if he was inching closer to the first one, then the second one. We compared notes with other parents who had typical babies, and each time I heard their child had reached a milestone, I cringed if Owen hadn't. At the same time, he was beginning to write his own success story.

When Owen was two months old, we met his first physical therapist, Margaret, who showed up at our house on a Friday morning, her dancing blue eyes filled with warmth as she introduced herself. I offered her a cup of coffee and we bonded over our Irish heritage. It became our Friday ritual, sitting in the den with our steaming cups of coffee, Owen contentedly playing on the floor in pajamas that were too big for his little body. I felt like I had found a friend in this new world, someone who assured me that everything was going to be okay. After her first session with Owen, I walked her to her car. My fragility was apparent, both as a new mom and now a mom to a child with special needs.

"What do you think?" I asked tentatively. "About Owen?" Her eyes lit up.

"I think he's amazing! He's already doing so well in the way he tracks toys and holds up his neck. To be honest, he's ahead of the curve." I hugged her spontaneously, needing so badly to connect with someone who could help me navigate and understand this uncharted territory. She was a trained specialist from the world of special needs, and like the Good Witch of the East, Margaret had dropped into my life to help me find my own way back on the yellow brick road.

I tripped over my words as I poured out my story. I told her about the week of not knowing and how our unwitting ignorance turned into a nightmare. Given her Irish background, I told her what my doctor had said to me. It was a follow-up visit in his office when, after my exam, he closed the door and asked me with a soothing kindness if I was okay. I couldn't help myself as I began to weep; it was a long, dark release in front of someone who I trusted with my baby and his birth. It didn't occur to me my tears and dark mood could possibly be from the hormones.

"It's a shame when your guardian angel decides to take the day off, isn't it?" he said gently, his hand on my shoulder. His words and manner soothed me, but in hindsight I have come to believe that my angel hadn't taken a day off. Instead, my guardian angel was sent to participate in my life, rooted in my son's body, showing me that the physical disability was merely the vessel he inhabited.

I became obsessed with counting the signs that didn't exist: there was no palmar crease on the palm of his hand. His ears weren't set lower than his eyes. He didn't have wide-set eyes or a fused pinky toe. He didn't have a curved pinky finger. He had no major heart problems or intestinal problems. Then I noted the signs he did have: slanted eyes, a crease on the top of his ear, iris brush spots, a big space between his big toe and second toe—although his dad had that too—and feet that looked like a baby duck because he was so flatfooted. What I didn't count, and would add as he grew, was an increased stubbornness—as moms, we all noted that it had to be a part of the extra gene—a wicked sense of humor, and love that has no conditions.

Chapter Eleven

For the first few months, I hunkered down at home, reluctant to let new relationships bloom because we were just a mom and her baby, getting to know each other. Friends and family rallied around me, wanting to visit, wanting to meet him, asking how I was doing. I was fine, I reassured everybody. Inside, though, the gnarled parts of me still felt cheated, and every smile I hid behind was a constant fight not to collapse into my own house of mirrors. As intently as I studied my son, I avoided studying myself with the same fervor. I refused to go inward and analyze why this was such a blow to me, to my ego. Innately, I felt as if I had failed in some way—failed at producing a perfect child. Yet I never questioned what my ideal of perfection was. Had I defined perfection early in my childhood when I was sorting through who I was? Had my ideals become so high that I couldn't make room for a glitch or an error in nature's computation?

Everywhere I went, all I saw were babies the same age as Owen; they sprung up like wildflowers. I'd spot them at Target, at the bank, on my walks. It's as if I had opened up a gateway and every perfectly formed baby was set in my path. What I would learn as the days passed is that in a way, we were lucky to know Owen's diagnosis so early so we could face it head-on. I met parents during my son's life who found out their child had a disability much later, something they weren't prepared for since they were already walking down the path marked "typical." As the years went on, it became a calling card, and my phone often rang with a parent who passed along another parent who had a child diagnosed with a disability. My friends and I jokingly called it "the coolest club you never wanted to join" because we met so many amazing, hardworking, intense, honest, and broken parents. We shared the same sadness and the same hopes and dreams for our children.

At six months old, an occupational therapist came to evaluate Owen. Erik introduced her to Owen, who was sitting in his high chair, ready for breakfast. A pile of Cheerios sat on the tray in front of him, and he slowly lifted them one by one to his mouth. His little fingers grasped the tiny circle, then sucked on it until it was soft enough to swallow.

"He can eat Cheerios by himself?" she asked, a little puzzled.

"Of course," said Erik, who worked incessantly with Owen on teaching him to feed himself. "He's about to eat breakfast. Do you want to watch?"

"Why? Does he do tricks?" She laughed.

"Okay, Owen," Erik said excitedly. "It's time for breakfast. Can you help your daddy out?" He put a bowl of baby oatmeal in front of Owen and raised the spoon. Owen grabbed it, put the oatmeal in his mouth, swallowed it, then lowered the spoon. Erik smiled and congratulated Owen as his tiny feet kicked the air in excitement. The therapist looked at us.

"I know typical babies who can't do that," she said, a tinge of confusion in her voice.

Erik smiled. "They gave us reading material on what Down syndrome kids can and cannot do. I didn't read it. I just decided we would try everything a typical kid can do, but earlier." I listened from the other room as this exchange happened, desperate to leave for work so I wouldn't be late. But hearing the admiration apparent in her voice caused me to rejoice inside. Another victory. *I'll take the win*, I thought.

Soon after Margaret started working with Owen, she asked

me if I had heard of cranial sacral therapy (CST), which she had been studying. It's a type of bodywork that relieves compression in the bones of the head, sacrum, and spinal column. She told me it is often used on babies who were born via C-section, and it possibly might help Owen in other ways as it could potentially help him fire up neurons and improve his cognitive function. I was deeply intrigued. One morning, instead of our usual therapy, Margaret brought a CST-trained therapist who was skilled in revisiting childbirth to help complete an interrupted birth story.

The woman asked about my C-section and Owen's positioning. She was very serious and didn't smile. Upon her request, I positioned him on a blanket, face down, and she began lightly touching points on his body. He started to get fussy, then began all-out crying. She picked him up and held him as I explained to her how he was positioned in my womb: upside down, his face forward to the front of my belly. As Owen continued to cry, she slowly took him through the whole birth process again, lightly touching certain areas of his body to help him elongate his bones and muscles while turning him around in a spiral as if he were progressing down the birth canal. He was crying so loudly and continuously that I was a little worried. Yet as I sat next to her, I felt as if I was experiencing his birth again, with him. It was a strange and intriguing moment we shared.

The CST practitioner explained that because of his positioning in my womb, there was compression on his spine, and without the opportunity to come down the birth canal, to "decompress," there was a lot of tension. This explained why he had such tight neck muscles, and a bump had developed on the opposite side of his head. Our pediatrician assumed it had come from sleeping on a preferred side.

"For every action there is a reaction," the woman explained. "And with the buildup of tension, it has appeared as a bump in his cranium." She continued holding him, allowing him to guide her hands as he reached for an imaginary outlet. This went on for about twenty minutes until he twisted his neck and pointed downward. Afterward, she guided him into my lap. Instantly, he fell asleep, calmer than I had seen him before. She looked at me with a steady assuredness.

"He'll sleep soundly for a long time. He needs it." When she left my house, I turned to Margaret in awe.

"I am amazed at how instinctive Owen was," I said. She smiled knowingly. To me, it felt as if he and I had completed his birth journey.

I was a believer from that point on and found a licensed CST therapist named Jennifer, who dealt only with babies, some as young as an hour old, many of them with disabilities. I immediately felt a connection with her. She was like a therapist for me, often coaxing me to talk about the insecurities and fears I had. She assured me that Owen would change the world one day, in his own way, but I could not fathom how this little creature would do that in all his perceived brokenness.

I asked one day if I could try CST with her, to understand what Owen was feeling. There was no way for me to gauge how it was affecting him, except that he slept exceptionally well after every session. She agreed. As I lay on the table, her touch no heavier than the weight of a nickel, she listened to my body's rhythms and the flow of fluid through the nervous system, which is the core of cranial sacral therapy. If she found a "blockage," she massaged it. As she worked around my body, she came to my pelvic region and stopped, her hands hovering. She mentioned my organs were not sitting correctly, which was probably the result of how the doctor repositioned them after the C-section. (A faint smile played on the edge of her lips when I confirmed it was a male doctor.) She lay her hands on the area where my scar was, and I felt a deep warmth penetrating into my pelvis.

"Are you creating that heat?" I asked.

"Nope, you are. My hands are just above your body. I'm not even touching you." I looked down the length of my body to see her hands hovering above my pelvic region. After an hour, she finished. When I sat up, my entire body was buzzing.

"You are perfectly in sync right now," she said. "And for the next few days, you'll have a lot of clarity and ability to get things done."

Sure enough, my productivity soared in every project I completed. I felt as if I were carrying a secret around as I looked at the world around me with renewed interest. Nature seemed more glorious than before. I felt strong and empowered. I settled into my new reality a bit more and wondered how I had not known about this treatment before now. How had I only now stumbled into a world of treatment that lived between the spaces of belief? Owen's response to the treatment was less visible. I sometimes wondered if it was doing anything at all, but after my experience, I knew that changes were happening inside of him that we weren't aware of, and perhaps might never be able to gauge.

Chapter Twelve

"What about Owen?" Erik asked one night over dinner. Those three words reminded me that I had entered this brave new world of parenthood where the youngest member of the tribe is the most important. Selfishness isn't allowed anymore when you have a baby.

"If you return to work, we can put him in daycare like every other working family does," I said bravely, aware that I had already sorted this out in my mind, not understanding the problem. Owen was a baby, just like any other baby. Erik was uncomfortable with my answer, I could tell, but put the conversation aside. At the time, the project he and his dad had been working on was the house we moved into. Technically, the house had been finished, and there was no new project on the horizon. Secretly, I didn't understand why we were even having the conversation. He was home. I had a steady income with benefits. And even though our child had a disability, it didn't render him unable to go to daycare or any other babysitting alternative. But I wasn't thinking from Erik's point of view. I had no idea what he thought, as my tendency was to embroil myself in my internal lines of reasoning, dreaming up every scenario until I finally decided what would work. Our communication had been solely focused on taking each day as it came, managing our baby's health, and pointedly not discussing anything outside of that realm. For me, I knew I could default to the safety of my job, where order and surety prevailed.

The insular days of maternity sped by, and I both dreaded and anticipated the return to work. The impending return date added another layer of anxiety at the thought of leaving the hormone-soaked days of feedings, naps, and newborn nuzzles for editorial meetings and long commutes. As a mother, I had not only witnessed the miracle of life; I had been the vehicle through which this tiny form had taken shape and sprung forth into my universe. As the days went by, just like my postpartum belly, my world began to return to its previous shape. I always intended to return to work, but now, with this new diagnosis plugged into my world, it felt even more important to me. I needed that anchor, even if it only meant an office to sit in, conversation with my colleagues, and an opportunity to untangle my thoughts as I concentrated on whatever task was at hand.

To say I was proud of my badge of motherhood was also a misnomer. I was confused as to what I should think, or say, or do. I was transformed by his birth, slayed by his diagnosis, and afraid to return to the life I had built without having some kind of script. My doctor had offered me pills for anxiety, but I refused. Instead, I chased after the natural high, walking countless miles with Owen either in a stroller or snuggled in a baby Bjorn. The walks gave me time to think, to process. In the span of three months, on top of the layer of being a new mom, I suddenly had to open up my home to new people and news experiences, adding layers of medical paperwork. I almost longed for the simplicity of my day job. There were moments when I craved a bit of the life I had before becoming a parent.

I had gone from a woman refusing to cancel a meeting because I was in labor, to a brief stint as a stay-at-home mom. The glimpse into that life was jarring, and perhaps it was because of the extra mental and physical demands. I didn't know any other new mom who had to host a therapist once a week, sort through a new list of timelines and milestones, and enroll her baby in a state organization called the Department of Developmental Services for lifetime benefits. Perhaps they were out there, hidden like me, dealing with a diagnosis, and struggling to normalize their lives.

One thing I did know was that I wasn't ready to be home full-time. I missed the life I had built before I had a baby. As much as I loved Owen, I was unnerved by the weight of being a parent of a special needs child. There were hints of hard work ahead—and little did I understand how every baby entailed hard work—but more important to me at the moment was to regain a semblance of normality, to take back the life I had carved out before Owen was born.

During the first few months of Owen's life, Erik and I were at a bit of a stalemate about what the scenario looked like when I went back to work, because in my mind, there was no other choice. I had taken a new position when I was six months pregnant, with the caveat that I was going back after maternity leave. My contract included full salary while I was home on the condition I return after three months. Somewhere deep within me, I knew going back might help me gain a bit of objective clarity and restore my self-confidence. Working in public relations allowed me the ability to control the outcome of any event or story. It was all in the planning, and if I did my job correctly, even when something went wrong, nobody noticed. I couldn't control the genetic outcome of my child, but I could control my work, and gaining back a little control in my spiraling mind was the impetus for me to go back. An integral part of PR was to learn how to spin any story. My story needed its own spin to sell it to myself; my family and my friends had all accepted the reality.

Somewhere, somehow, our communication channel had been affected, and the few times I mentioned going back to work, I was met with stony silence. My plan all along had been to return to work, but with the pain and heartache of Owen's diagnosis, I had overlooked the key ingredient that would help me transition smoothly: connection. I hadn't conveyed to Erik that to me this diagnosis was merely a bump in the road; it wasn't going to change the future I had so carefully built.

The first day back to work was chaos in our household, as I assumed it must be for thousands of mothers who return to work three months after giving birth. I awoke early, but minutes get lost when you have to plan for a baby. My former routine was taking on a whole new dimension. Feed the baby, shower, get dressed, struggle to find clothes that fit a body shaped differently than it was before I got pregnant. A postpartum body is an ever-changing fight with gravity for those of us not born supermodels. I grabbed all the things I needed for the day: computer, phone, and now a breast pump with attachments. I was lucky if I had time to make lunch to take with me. Flustered, I kissed the baby and my husband goodbye and drove back into the life of a working mom.

I tried to quell my nervousness, using the long drive as a pep talk to myself. I had birthed a baby despite the complications (yay, me!) and completed another adult milestone. I was a dues-paying member of the parenthood club.

The receptionist greeted me with a sweet smile. She had been with the company for close to thirty years, and we often spoke of children and her grandchildren. She asked how the baby was.

"He has Down syndrome," I blurted, not anticipating the suddenness with which I would have to answer the question. She stood up and gave me a hug.

"You'll be a great mom."

A few colleagues knew of Owen's diagnosis before I came back to work. One night during maternity leave, I was at dinner with my husband and some friends. I had chosen a restaurant where I wouldn't run into anyone I knew. Unfortunately, just as we sat down, I spotted my colleagues having dinner. I cringed, not wanting to spoil my maternity leave quite yet. There had been whispers—rumors—among my community of coworkers, but nobody knew for sure yet. I couldn't bear them silently pitying me. I didn't want to invite the world in until I had to. Erik told me to leave it alone and act like I never saw them. But that wasn't my nature. I took a deep breath and went over to their table.

"Hey, guys," I said, a big grin pasted on my face. They responded with questions about the baby. Not sure what my answer should be, I blurted it out.

"My son was diagnosed with Down syndrome." They looked at

me for a moment, unsure what to say, until one of them locked eyes with me.

"Hey, kid, I bet it's hard. I get it. I don't know if you heard, but my son died recently. Drugs. Be glad you have a child who won't walk that path."

I was taken aback. I had no idea. I gave him a quick hug.

"Thank you," I whispered and then went back to my seat where the laughter was flowing as easily as the wine, and we ate and drank up those stolen moments away from our baby. It dawned on me that this new reality was mine to own; the birth of my child, and his diagnosis, were drawing people and their stories to me—stories I might never have known. I was now part of the mechanism of a goodness I had not anticipated, a truthfulness the world was reluctant to see, in the form of a baby who would one day teach more compassion to friends and family than I could even anticipate. I was more prepared at that moment than I had ever been to face what I thought was going to be the battle of society: suiting up as a warrior mom whose son didn't fit society's mold, who was the poster child for termination. His comment made me realize that we all fight our own battles; nobody is exempt. I didn't have any choice but to go forward, to begin again. *I can do this* resonated deep within the spaces inside of me, and I did.

From then on, I told everyone who crossed my path that Owen had Down syndrome: the mailman, the crossing guard, the grocery store clerk, friends, friends of friends, our softball team, and the gas station attendant. I told anyone who looked my way because I wanted to control the conversation, to forestall the odd looks, to anticipate the "I'm sorry" or the "too bad." I did it to prepare myself for those people whose comments were hurtful or ignorant. They existed like trolls under a bridge, and every time I heard a new phrase, I cringed. "Didn't you test?" was a constant question. "I think they call them Mongoloids," was another statement I heard, in a grocery store while I was shopping for baby food. "I heard they don't live very long. Good luck," was another response, which made me run for a quiet place as fast as I could to sob until I had no more tears left. It was my way of pressing forward, of being proactive instead of reactive. If I intuited which way the conversation was going, I could manage it.

I was shopping with Cynthia one day when I told another random person about my beautiful little boy and his genetic diagnosis. After the encounter, she turned to me, confused.

"You know, it's a little odd how you tell every single person you meet about Owen's diagnosis." I looked at her, knowing her observation came from a place of love, but I reminded her that this was my way of grieving, of getting through it and not dancing around it.

I recall the nights he lay sleeping when the house was silent except for the refrigerator's hum and the occasional beep of the dryer alerting me that the tiny baby clothes he went through so frequently were dry. I recall watching his even, soft breathing as the black night sky pressed against the windows. Those moments in the middle of the night, after I fed him and his eyes were closed, drunk with sleep, calmed me. His perfect eyebrows that kids with Down syndrome are gifted with, tinged a golden red, and his chest rising ever so slightly brought a contentedness I had never known. This defines motherhood: the brief moments when you know your child will never be this little, this perfect, this close to you, and you feel that moment with every cell in your body. You feel ions of love emanating between the two of you, and it sustains you for another day, another night. I wish I could freeze these moments to unwrap later in my life, these wisps of time when nobody could say anything damaging to me, nobody could infuse their own beliefs on me, nobody could disturb what I had rightfully earned: my baby's softness, his aliveness, his measured breath as he slept.

But he grew, as did I. We both were about to enter new stages, his more physical than mine. Looking back at what I learned about babies and growth, I know now that when he learned to crawl, it took more neurons and mental coordination than we understand. The building blocks that we, as humans, develop when we are young determine our capacity for growth as adults. I watched my child unfold in a slower manner. He learned to army crawl first and didn't walk until he was almost two years old. But having the best seat in the house, a front-row view to watch how nature's mechanics work, is a wondrous opportunity. My growth was internal and matched the five stages of grief: denial, anger, bargaining, depression, and acceptance. They were all somehow muddled together, and I couldn't denote a linear path. But at different times of the day or week, I would find myself sunk in one of those categories. Denial was in my eyes as I watched him grow and dared to hope the doctors were wrong, that we would get a call any day now with the apology that the test was meant for another family. Anger lived with me constantly, a slow burn that simmered as I railed against the universe for trusting that I could handle this diagnosis. I didn't bargain, but if I could have found a deal to make with the devil to take back that extra chromosome, you bet I would have sold my soul to do it. Depression was the sneakiest; it would creep up on me at the oddest times and suck out any energy I had to sustain the breakneck speed with which I was racing through my life. I always believed if I worked faster, I could get to the finish line before anyone else. The problem was that the line was constantly moving, always just a few more steps or miles out of reach. And what was my end game anyway? I was in constant motion, never stopping unless I had to. Busyness was a badge of honor for me. But it would take years before I realized acceptance was what waited at the finish line. Acceptance was about letting go, and to do that, I would have to relinquish control, which I wasn't yet ready to do.

Chapter Thirteen

When I was age twenty-two, I was set on my goal of leaving Michigan and moving to Los Angeles. I relished the freedom of setting out across the country. Everything I deemed valuable in my life was reduced to the dimensions of my Chevrolet's trunk. During college, I had driven a van for work eight hours a day all across the state of Michigan, traveling over bridges and through remote towns, stopping at drugstores to bring the bulging bags of Kodak disposable cameras back for processing. Nothing unnerved me—certainly not driving. So experiencing panic attacks while driving completely threw me off.

I can't remember my first panic attack. I only know that after a few had occurred, I could finally define them. I don't think anyone envisions a life that has to make space for panic attacks. I never thought about the day when they became an added element. That moment when all control was superseded by clammy hands, shortness of breath, and the desperate inability to control my emotions, thoughts, or actions. Anxiety and panic attacks are cousins, resembling each other closely but with notable distinctions. A panic attack crescendos in one horrendous, compressed moment in time; anxiety, on the other hand, lies in wait, buzzing under the surface of daily life as it clamps its mighty hands on my rational brain. I had dealt with anxiety all my life; it was almost a natural state of being for me. If I was anxious and thought hard enough about what was not working out, then nothing was ever as bad as the scenario I had created in my mind. It was a fool's way to live, wasting each moment with a hyped-up idea of senseless doom. Call it Catholic guilt, but I believed that being in a state of constant worry protected me from the actual event happening. Why? Because, of course, it all comes back to control. Letting my mind dictate what might happen by envisioning it first created a sense of preparedness, yet all that ever transpired was a big, fat panic attack. All thoughts led back to control. At this juncture in my life, I had no control over my baby's birth, his chromosomes, and what his life would look like. I could only anticipate his needs, then guide him. But I struggled with how to keep my world in check without constantly being rooted in control mode.

I thought keeping myself busy all the time could alleviate some of the panic, but I was unsure how to conquer the demons that sat on my shoulder, waiting for the ideal moment to pounce. I didn't have time to address solutions, so I parked that Post-it note— "Work on self!" —in the back of my mind.

When Owen was six months old, we visited a program at UCLA for babies and toddlers with special needs. I took the morning off to check it out with Erik and Owen. Tucked away in a corner of the campus, I breathed in the collegiate energy that surrounded us as we walked by students grouped together, chatting and laughing. Years ago, I worked in Westwood at Time Inc. Magazines, which was conveniently located across the street from UCLA. Many nights after work I'd stroll over to the campus track and walk until it grew dark, pausing to take in the enormity that I lived in LA and worked so close to a school I had admired and dreamed of since I was in junior high. I eventually enrolled in night classes there because I loved learning and I had the time (read: no kids yet!). Not to mention the fact that UCLA had a vast assortment of highly qualified teachers who taught extension courses. Back then, newly minted to LA and a bit homesick for my family, I was even more homesick for college life, so I basked in the

Chapter Thirteen • 71

university life, walking miles around campus just to be immersed in the energy of the students and academia in general.

Now I'd taken on a vastly different mission, so many years and worlds away from my college days. Arriving at UCLA for nonacademic reasons on this morning had me a bit discombobulated, to say the least. We entered a large room filled with babies and toddlers of all ages and engaged in various play stations. Adults worked with some of the kids, while others were playing freely. I marveled at the foresight of UCLA to create this daycare incubator where therapists working on their studies at UCLA had access to babies and toddlers with special needs. It was a win/win for everyone.

I sat Owen down in front of a pile of toys and wandered around. Erik stayed on the other side of the room, and I saw him pull the director aside and whisper to her. The woman nodded, then left.

"What was that about?" I asked, my eyes on Owen across the room, who was contentedly playing with the toys in front of him. I never had to worry about attachment anxiety. Owen didn't seem bothered if we placed him amidst adult "strangers" or with kids he didn't know. Ironically, he had no anxiety, barely cried, and never seemed to exhibit any kind of distress. Had I been looking for signs, I might have seen even then that he had a Zen way of living in his world, which was so opposite of my nature. "Wherever I go, there I am" was a statement that often came to my mind. It was a frightful statement if I applied it to myself, but so perfectly apt when I applied it to Owen.

"I thought she might have a resource for you . . . maybe a therapist. I told her it's been really hard on you. She said she has someone you can talk to who she highly recommends." I paused, confronted yet again with myself and my inability to process something this overwhelming. I fought back tears, not wanting to capitulate to another round of crying.

I inhaled a deep breath. I had to agree with Erik. There was no way I could climb this mountain by myself. Still, I was irritated by his suggestion and the proactive choice he made to ask around for help on my behalf. For me, the angst of finding someone and actually showing up was a harder pill to swallow. If I looked closely, though, I could see that it was his way of showing how much he cared about me and the family we had created. It was time to own up to my own personal demons. The director came back with a name and number.

"Hey, it's okay. Everybody needs someone to talk to sometimes," she assured me. "I highly recommend this woman. Years ago, she worked with a group of moms who had kids with Down syndrome. From what I heard, they loved working with her." As we left UCLA, I felt a glimmer of hope mixed with a hint of fear, knowing this was possibly the next, most necessary step for me.

I didn't call. Not that day, or the next, or the next one hundred days. I kept putting it off, even going so far as to hide the number in a drawer. Maybe all my issues would magically resolve and I wouldn't need to make the call.

For months, I randomly opened the drawer, pulled out the piece of paper, held it up, held my breath, then stuck it right back in the drawer on an exhale. The act of calling that number and confronting the voice on the other end to make an appointment was a bigger mental hurdle than I'd imagined.

I tried support groups first at the urging of Owen's therapists, and Erik took the lead on it. He went down a list of numbers for support groups, looking for someone to help us navigate our new life with a special needs child. One woman he talked to had him shaking his head. The conversation started by Erik asking about the support group.

"Can you tell me a little bit about it? Where does it meet? How many people attend?" She interrupted him with a shout to one of her kids.

"Stop doing that! I told you once already. Sorry," she responded. "I'm not really involved in the group anymore. I don't have time with three kids, and they are a lot of work." Again, she shouted something at one of her kids.

"Do you mind me asking, is it your child with Down syndrome who is a lot of work?" Erik asked.

"Oh no, he's just sitting here, quietly playing. It's my two typical kids who are driving me crazy."

After he got off the phone, he turned to me and said, "I really don't think it's a bad thing we have a child with Down syndrome. That woman sounded so overwhelmed. I think we have a great little boy here."

On good days, I kept that perspective, and the diagnosis didn't seem so bad. Other days, ominous statistics scrolled through my head like the Wall Street Stock Exchange: a greater percentage develop early childhood leukemia while fifty percent are born with heart defects, vision problems, hearing issues, feeding issues. How much should I pay attention to? When I bathed him, I would scan his body for any little mark or bruise that might indicate leukemia. I watched his eyes follow objects intently, looking for the least bit of crossing in his pupils. I tested his hearing in my own subtle ways by coming around a corner and calling his name. And I tried every food possible for a baby so I could watch as he mastered them one by one. We set no limits because we wanted him to be limitless. We cheered when he beat any Down syndrome statistic: sitting up at six months, crawling at ten months, and potty-trained at twenty-two months before he even started walking.

But how much of the statistics do you pay attention to, and where does your child fall? It's as if the medical community sets us up for failure by giving us numbers to follow, saying your child will do this but not that, and make sure you aren't disappointed when he doesn't do something by a certain age. For me, coming from a competitive family but also realizing we live in an age of competitiveness, with parents constantly comparing their kids to other kids, it was hard to realize that I had been given a different measuring stick. At the end of the day, though, I believed somewhere deep inside my core—and no statistic can tell me differently—that my son would be brilliant in his own way and have a good and fulfilling life.

Chapter Fourteen

My panic attacks became more frequent and more intrusive. I was consumed by the inability to control my world. Driving home from work I was okay one minute, then the next moment I couldn't breathe and would feel almost dizzy. It would last a few seconds, but it was enough time for me to pay attention. My hands broke out with eczema, and I scratched until they were bloody. The angry welts oozed and swelled until I couldn't even wear my wedding ring. Some days I sat at my desk as horrible scenarios befalling Erik and Owen at home would take over my mind: a car accident, a choking incident, a drowning, or some unnamed virus would attack. If Erik didn't call me back right away on his cell, my panic grew, and the visions would take on a life of their own, expanding like a balloon filled with air. If I could only learn to let the balloons of terror float away, wafting off to another land where they could slowly deflate. But that's not how my mind worked; it was a coping skill I had never learned to implement, since that would mean letting go of the one thing I could—falsely—count on: control.

One morning, I couldn't leave for work. Distraught and panicked, I tried to tell Erik what I was feeling, but all I could do was weep. I was so overcome by these visions that something bad was going to happen. Calmly, Erik reassured me that he was completely capable of taking care of Owen.

"It's not that," I said through my tears. "It's just that I think something else bad is going to happen because it already did. We are no longer exempt. Bad things happen to good people, and they keep happening. What makes us any different?"

Erik hugged me. "I think it's time you call that therapist, the one who deals with people like us."

Getting the appointment was easy; showing up was hard. There is something harrowing about walking into a therapist's office. You know nothing about this person but assume they already think you are screwed up. A part of me felt ashamed, as if I had done something wrong to necessitate the need to see a therapist. I lived under the illusion that therapy meant I couldn't manage my life. I had to see this as different, though, in order to show up. I needed to address my mental health in a situation that I was not prepared for. If I was going to be the mother my son needed, I had to leave my preconceived notions at the door and enter.

The waiting room was dim with neutral walls and a faded brown couch. There were three doors, each closed, and a red buzzer was shining. The sign indicated to press the button upon arrival, so I did, then sat on the tired-looking couch, nervous, sweating under my shirt. I wanted to run away, to bolt, to find the nearest coffee shop and sit for the duration. Nothing is more excruciating than the wait, when your mind turns over every awful thing you have ever done in your life and presents it to you in stark, black-and-white images that parade back and forth in your mind's eye.

Within a few minutes, an elderly woman, her face framed by frizzled gray hair and owl-like glasses, opened the door. She introduced herself as Dr. Nancy Miller and invited me in. Her office was an attempt at cheeriness that was ageless: a soft, worn, brown teddy bear sat propped on the couch, while a few toys littered the carpet, and a crocheted blanket lay folded over a chair upon which a sunny pillow with gray felt letters spelled out "Life is good." She noticed my eyes on the toys and explained parents occasionally bring their kids with them. I gingerly picked a seat on the couch, away from the bear, and sat awkwardly. She was kind, and as we began to chat, albeit slowly, she told me about the group of moms she led in a focus group years ago who had kids with Down syndrome. She handed me a copy of her book *Nobody's Perfect: Living and Growing with Children Who Have Special Needs*. Her gentle voice lulled me into a sense of relief; finally, someone already understood what Down syndrome was, and I didn't have to spend an hour educating her.

Soon enough, I could feel tears slipping down my cheeks, and I began the long, hard sobbing that came so easily to me these days. Between tears, I told her about my fears, my thoughts, and my desperation to understand "why me?" She listened, handing me a tissue between words, and I finally felt safe enough to express the anger, the ugly words that lingered in my mind, without being judged. I had been judging myself for too many months, and now it was time to release the thoughts so they could dissipate and not claim so much power over me. They were my dirty little secrets, and I was powerless to stop them from coming out. Comforting and blameless, she was a soft landing for what had been a hard journey.

As my therapy sessions progressed, Dr. Miller pulled my fears apart one by one. She reminded me of how far I had come in my life, of my successes. I liked her positive attitude, her ease with which she embraced the facts of my life, and she helped me see some of it as just that: facts. The things that cannot be changed because they just are. "Write down your fears," she urged me, "so you can learn to laugh at how absurd they are. Bad things happen, but not all bad things happen to one person." She asked me to embrace my new reality instead of pushing it away. And as I began to face it head-on, some of the hostile energy that kept me spinning around like the Tasmanian devil subsided a bit. I could exhale more easily.

I still had a lot of mental cleaning up to do from the earlier parts of my life, since therapy doesn't just open one tiny bit, like regulating a dam; it lets the floodgates open wide. She wrestled my earlier demons out of me: the low self-esteem, the perfectionism, and the need to control. She didn't judge, and she didn't question. She simply played the part of listener, trying to put the puzzle pieces together and help me solve the reason I was here now.

After a few sessions, she laid out a new card on the table. She wanted Erik to join us the following week. Fear immediately seized me. This was my safe space where all my demons were exhumed. Did I dare let him in? How do you tell your husband and the father of your baby that he is not allowed into the sanctity marked "private"? How do you reconcile that the life you once lived and the wrong turns you chose are something you definitely, absolutely, under no circumstance want anyone to know about? But she knew the power in her asking, and reluctantly, I admitted him.

My terror came from the thought that my therapist would expose all my secrets, even though my practical mind knew she wouldn't. By introducing my husband into my secret world of damage, I was opening myself up to a vulnerability I wasn't quite ready to expose. But there was the possibility that he needed to be heard too; that he was struggling in his own way and would benefit from her insight.

When we arrived, I set Owen down and he became engaged with the toys. She started out by asking how things were going, and I explained my recent feelings: the idea that Owen had been sent to challenge my life, as if God was sending a really big message to nudge me to live my life differently. Sometimes I had visions of what my life would be like if I took the plunge: quit my job and started writing. My fear was tied up in the failure I thought I could foresee, but now I was starting to think that Owen had already nudged me off the ledge. In society's eyes, I had already failed to produce a "perfect" child, so what did I have to lose now?

Dr. Miller turned to Erik, cutting to the chase. "What do you think about the idea that your wife thinks she didn't have the 'perfect' child?"

He sat there for a moment, smiling. "I don't think my son is a failure. I disagree with how she thinks about him; I think he's perfect. Look, we got pregnant, and out of the millions of sperm that could have been any child, he won the race. He made it and won the prize of life, and he was born. That's pretty incredible to me."

I looked at him, stunned. I had never seen it that way. Despite what I perceived as Owen's brokenness, he was the winner. He beat out any other child who could have been typical, and he survived. Erik's way of thinking was so resolute, so sure. He never wavered when it came to Owen. He believed from the moment Owen was born that he was perfect. And yet, his optimism about Owen made me feel inferior, that if I, his own mother, couldn't muster up the same attitude, something must be wrong with me. That conversation stuck with me. I was seeing chinks in my belief system. The overwhelming thought that I had done something wrong was slowly dissolving. Erik's sense of absolute—that Owen was meant to be who he is, and that he was meant to be our son—was infiltrating my locked attitude, giving me pause.

I began to regain my sense of place in the universe, trusting a little more each day that there was a guiding force leading all things. There was a reason Owen was sent to us, and a reason he didn't die in childbirth. I felt as if an invisible hand was telling the story and we were the puppets. After his diagnosis, I was often confronted by blunt—aka rude—people who asked loaded questions: "Does it run in your family?" (That has no bearing because it's a totally random error during cell division). "Were you careful with what you ate and drank?" Or my favorite, "You know there's a test for that, right?" I almost wanted to slap my hand to my forehead and say, "Really? Wow, you are so much smarter than me! How did I not know I could choose prenatal testing when I spent nine months pregnant, reading every book?" The idiocy of people should have made me laugh, but it often made me cry.

Yet their questions challenged my core belief that I was so steadfast in when I became pregnant: whoever we are gifted with is our child, and nothing can change that. It's easy, in theory, to stay strong in your morals and declare your truth. But when people start to chip away at that foundation, to open your eyes to another point of view, an alternate ending to the story, it's hard not to waver in your beliefs and explore what that alternative means. At the end of the day, though, my moral compass always pointed to the life we had created, the new little one who was now ours to love and to learn from.

One Sunday morning, I had the urge to clear away any misgivings. "What would you have done if I had taken the test?" I asked Erik outright. He paused, knowing exactly what I was asking but unsure how to answer.

"I don't know," he said honestly. "I might have been that person to push you to terminate." I had always been so resolute in my awareness that I would not have terminated, but I had to remember there were two of us. Clearly, an invisible guide had played a part in our journey. What would we have done if we had found out? Either one of us might have been pressured by others to make a different choice, to let fear rule our decision. It may not be how we wanted the story to go, but it was our story, and we chose life. I always knew that I could not have lived my life with a different decision; regret would have darkened my life. Our child brought such joy into our lives, challenged us with a range of emotions, and infused in us a desire to mold him into the best person he could be. So we set out to prove we could help him bust through any negative clinical determination.

It would be nice to say that therapy tied everything up in a bow and handed me the gift of a life of happiness, devoid of anxiety or panic, but that was not the case. Anxiety ebbs and flows, and panic subsides. But having once experienced a panic attack, it can never be forgotten. I reached back into my past and traced my first panic attack back to a trip to Coronado Island, years before I met Erik. My youngest brother was in town, and we decided to explore Coronado, just south of San Diego, in what I thought would be a fun adventure. After all, I am the girl who drove across the country from Michigan to California without giving any forethought to panic. That day, as we ascended the bridge, I got about midway and felt a cold sweat come over me. For a moment, I thought I was going to pass out, and the movie played forward in my mind of the car driving off the bridge. I continued driving, my hands gripping the steering wheel as the curve of the narrow bridge bowed over the water to the island below. The moment passed, and I dismissed it. I didn't feel that way again until a few years later: I was heading into the Verdugo Hills and toward the overpass that had the same curved engineering. I felt my world tilt and a chill come over me. My mind raced again, wondering what the scenario would look like if I had passed out while driving. The moments began to add up like pearls on a necklace. If I looked ahead and saw a bridge or overpass that looked too high or curved out of sight, I panicked. I tried to keep these bits of my mind unraveling to myself, but it became more obvious as time went on. I bowed out of a trip to the mountains if it meant I had to drive curved mountain roads to get there. I avoided the overpasses that triggered my mind and instead found alternate routes, surface streets that led me to the next freeway on-ramp. It was beginning to affect my life. But like all good secrets, if you can find lies to cover them, then nobody will know the difference.

Therapy doesn't erase the parts you want to get rid of; instead, therapy asks you to face what you are avoiding head-on. But your mind will only unravel the roadblocks when you want to, when you are ready to unravel the knots of pain. I can never erase the memory of my panic attack, and I live with the knowledge that one can strike again at any moment, but I have given myself a few tools to help stem the tide of complete paralysis. My number-one tool is multiplying numbers out loud, starting with one times one—because math was never my best subject—and it forces me to really concentrate. Sadly, instead of thinking I can conquer the world, I want to hide from it, all while wondering if it stems from the deeply rooted belief that not having control makes me spin out of control.

Chapter Fifteen

When Owen was one year old, I became pregnant again, unsurprisingly. Many of my brothers and sisters had babies close together, and I saw that as the logical next step, besides the fact that I now desperately wanted a sibling for Owen. I had gotten pregnant so easily with him, and I felt justified now, as if finally the ship that was listing had righted itself, and I was on track for normalcy. I felt sure this one would be my typical child, allowing me to redeem myself in my own eyes, and in society's eyes.

It's crazy how one year of being a mom to a child with Down syndrome made me crave a normalcy that I watched other moms embrace. Internally, I had defined myself as "less than," or "not good enough." Owen's diagnosis chipped away at my self-esteem and detracted from my wholeness. I thought Down syndrome was something to be feared rather than accepted, and I was still struggling to accept the perfection of his being. I was not ready to explore that perhaps it was not about Owen being less than perfect; it was about my inability to have confidence in myself because I had to make room in my now-imperfect world for Owen. I had to edit my definition of perfect, surrendering control as he challenged and changed my beliefs. In reality, Owen is perfect; he's just a different kind of perfect, blessed in his extra-chromosome way. He was the perfect child for my personal development so that later on I could understand how the puzzle pieces fit together.

As my ten-week doctor's appointment to check the baby's heartbeat approached, I took the week off of work. I wanted to be home with Erik and Owen and enjoy this insular time when I could dream about the life we would have together with our new bundle of joy. It was all shattered when the ultrasound didn't show a heartbeat. Stunned, I didn't want to believe it at first. I spent the next few days thinking my doctor was wrong, unwilling to give up on this new life I was carrying inside of me. I felt sideswiped yet again by a medical diagnosis; it had only been one year ago I was given news I didn't want to hear.

My doctor told me to come back in a week. If there were no changes, he would do another ultrasound. My first thought was embarrassment, since we had already told his parents and my family. I knew Erik's mom would not be gentle with me. I could hear her barbed insults already haunting me, echoing in my mind. As for my family, no one had ever miscarried—that was spoken of —except my mom, who had nine live births out of eleven pregnancies. I was deeply offended at my body for betraying me not once, but twice. Neither of my sisters had experienced a miscarriage, let alone a child with a disability. My personal and physical credibility was shaken. I just couldn't get "creating a child" right. I chastised myself for taking a whole week off work; it now felt like wasted time in my mind. I knew I would spend the week in mental chaos, listing all the reasons in my head why I didn't deserve another baby.

A few days later, the miscarriage "theory"—*Maybe my doctor was wrong?*—inevitably became a reality, since hope alone cannot forestall what nature has put into motion. I had clung to a very small hope that the baby's heart was beating strong; perhaps it had been playing peek-a-boo during the ultrasound. Sometime in the middle of the night, I was jolted awake by a sudden urge to use the bathroom. I crept silently down the hallway, unwilling to turn on any lights to ensure I didn't wake Owen or Erik. I sat down on the toilet, praying, "Please, God, don't let this be it." Even in the dark,

I could feel the tiniest of something slide out of me. I glanced into the toilet and, by the light of the moon, saw a dark clump of blood knotted together. It was no bigger than a quarter, and I didn't know whether to flush or not. I sat back down as tears slowly slid down my face, and I wept for the baby I would never know. After what seemed like an hour, I got up, flushed the toilet and went back to bed. I couldn't sleep though. My eyes gazed out the window at the Hollywood Hills, the palm trees swaying in the night air. I had come so far and still had so far to go in my life. Memories assailed me, but at long last, I closed my eyes and fell asleep.

This was blow number two. Were all my eggs cracked? Nothing made me feel more broken than the realization I was unable to produce a child who was perfectly normal. I could barely get out of the starting gate with the second pregnancy. Despite my brain knowing it was nature's way of expelling what would not survive, I felt as if God were playing a joke on me. After all, I had been raised in a family of nine kids, with forty-five first cousins. How was it possible that I could not succeed at getting pregnant again, especially as I listened to my siblings joke about how easy it was for them? There was no open forum for miscarriages in my family; and I hadn't heard of it happening in my extended family. I was the first, again. The banter touched a bitterness in me I had not acknowledged before, possibly brought on by the feast-or-famine aspect of my life. I was living in a famine mentality. I couldn't dine at the same table as them. They had finished the meal, and I was left with the scraps.

That weekend, my stoic nature prevailed. I charged ahead with a previously planned get-together with our friends at Erik's mother's house in Malibu. It was a group of friends we had collected over the years, and we were all celebrating a milestone: one year as parents. Our babies were born in the span of a few months, and we leaned on each other as new moms. As our kids approached their first birthdays, we collectively agreed to meet for a "baby day reunion." When I made the plans, I had no idea I would be in the middle of a miscarriage, but I was not going to cancel. Eva barely remarked when I told her I had lost—rather, was in the process of losing—the baby. I think she would have disapproved if I had canceled the event.

"Well, it wasn't meant to be," she said offhandedly as I artfully arranged a vegetable platter for the guests. That was all she said. No sympathy or a shoulder to cry on; nothing else was said about the miscarriage again.

I couldn't take my doctor's advice to "go easy" because that wasn't my nature. "You're like a shark. If you stop moving, you die," Erik had often reminded me. He was right. When we got to Malibu, I took a three-mile walk by myself, breathing in the ocean air with tears rolling down my face as my unborn baby seeped out of me. I was determined not to let anyone know; it was my way of proving I was stronger than any ordeal God could throw at me. I refused to let this incident define me. I would not let my grief turn me away from these families with whom I so desperately wanted to feel I belonged. My life was becoming categorized, filed into groups determined by my child. Their babies were typical; Owen was not, so I hid my secret of miscarriage as we picnicked on blankets with our almost one-year-olds.

Inside, I was trying to process that I was a failure at getting pregnant with what I hoped would be a typical child, and I was too proud to admit that it bothered me. Just as I spent the first year of Owen's life donning a fake smile and cheery demeanor, I now carried it through the day as a badge of armor. Defiantly, I sipped on a glass of wine, watching our babies roll around as we set them all together on a picnic blanket. Wrapped up like baby burritos, from youngest to oldest, Owen was right in the middle—average height, average weight—donning an angelic smile. I loved him through my tears that day. When a friend sent us pictures a few weeks later of our infants lounging together, Owen's face was highlighted by a single beam of sunshine. Everyone who saw the picture noticed it, and it occurred to me that perhaps an angel had been sent to us. What if Owen was enough for our family and there would be no more children? But I wasn't ready to buy into the angel cliche—or the only-child deal.

From that day on, I doubled up my efforts to get pregnant. It was now a scientific challenge to me; there had to be a way to increase my odds of getting pregnant. I bought books, read blog posts, and charted my cycle, praying to God that this next month I'd be handed the gift of another pregnancy. It's only upon reflection that most insights come, and looking back at my angst about getting pregnant and my overzealous attention to it, of course another pregnancy wasn't going to happen immediately. I needed time to adjust, as did my body.

The months went on, and sometimes I randomly had a positive pregnancy test, but nothing that stuck. On the eve of my thirty-eighth birthday, we invited our friends Steve and Kelly, who had recently gotten married, over for dinner. They were deeply religious, and as we drank wine, the conversation turned to God and whether we considered Owen a gift—or a curse, as I was wont to think. I was still caught up in the frenzy of not being able to get pregnant, and I railed against my God for not listening to me or answering my prayers. After all, I had done what He asked and accepted Owen as my child. Why wasn't I allowed to have a second child? I felt so bitter that night, so full of hate for a God who had often seen me through dark times. Selfishly, it was all about me and my ability to prove that I could get pregnant and have a typical child. I was ready to kick and scream, so I threw a temper tantrum at God. If I couldn't have another child, then I could certainly act like one. Steve challenged me.

My voice quivered as I spoke. "I have done everything right. I have been a good person. And what do I get rewarded with? A son with Down syndrome and then a miscarriage. All I want is to have one more baby. Just one. Why is that so impossible? Everyone else around us seems to have no trouble getting pregnant and having babies born without disabilities."

"What if God has something better in store for you?" Steve asked. "He has a master plan for all of us. You just can't see it yet." I envied the sureness of his faith.

"Look at what an amazing family you have!" Steve's wife chimed in. "Look at that sweet little boy who has taught so many people, including us, about love and acceptance. That is God's gift. I understand that in this moment you can't see the fullness of the blessing Owen is and will become. But I can assure you one day it will be revealed to you. I can promise you that."

Erik came into the dining room during our conversation so Steve asked his opinion. "What do you think, Erik?" Having known him since childhood, Steve was aware Erik hadn't been raised with any religious background.

Erik thought for a moment. "You know, I never really believed in God because I don't believe in something you can't prove. But after Owen came into our lives, I have to believe there is something more. This little boy has brought such love and emotion into my life, and that's not something you can prove. But I can tell you it's real."

I looked at Erik, completely thrown off. He had been a staunch agnostic for as long as I had known him. For a moment, I thought he was drunk enough to be kidding, but his sincerity trumped my suspicion. You think you know someone, and then it's like they don a magician's hat and morph into someone else. It wasn't me who finally convinced him that the mystery of faith was real. It was Owen, who had been on this earth for only one year, who had led him to contemplate his own idea of faith.

"On that note," I said dramatically, "happy birthday to me, and may my wish come true." As I blew out the candle, I wished for the thousandth time that I would have a baby who would be genetically perfect and healthy. *Please, God. Amen.*

I sliced the cake that I had diligently spent the afternoon baking, feeling that my wish was futile, despite my pronouncement of faith. Yet a tiny seed of hope had indeed planted itself inside, buoyed by the fact that Erik had a glimmer of faith. I felt the pull of an invisible bond, which Owen had touched off in us, giving us the chance to look together into the future.

The next week I tested positive on a pregnancy test but refused to believe it would last. In my mind, this was no different than the last time, and the time before that. It took many more weeks until I finally trusted this was different, that it might actually work out. The pregnancy showered me with numerous fears, and I still doubted it was really going to "stick." I took a different approach this time and made an effort to implement more holistic practices.

I absolutely, completely, one hundred percent did not take this pregnancy for granted in any way. In fact, I was so afraid of another miscarriage that I didn't tell my family until I was fourteen weeks pregnant. By that time, we had seen a heartbeat, and initial ultrasounds showed the baby's growth was on target. With Owen, we didn't find out if he was a boy or girl because we felt there were so few surprises in life. And boy, were we surprised! With my second pregnancy, I wanted to know everything so there wouldn't be any surprises. The blood test proved I was having a girl. Delighted and a bit shocked, I said a quick prayer for the baby who I lost, since I always thought she was a girl.

Chapter Sixteen

In the early months when I was pregnant with Tess, despite my anxiety about her genetic makeup, I knew I was not going to have an amniocentesis. Yet this decision created negative scenarios in my head. One morning, as Margaret and I sipped our coffee while Owen played, she asked me if I had ever heard about Papa Joe and the Maoris. It vaguely rang a bell as she explained more about their practices and healings, and I realized another friend had also mentioned the Maoris and Papa Joe. Life was coming together in serendipitous ways. I found myself leaning in and asking more questions. The Maoris was a group from New Zealand, headed up by Papa Joe, who came to the US a few times a year. They were due to arrive in a few weeks. I eagerly signed up to join Margaret.

When we arrived at the beautiful Zen-like retreat in the hills of Topanga Canyon, several members of the Maori team were working with people, utilizing various massage techniques, and I heard people cry out in pain. A man came up and asked me who I was there to work with, and my voice stuck in my throat. I whispered, "Papa Joe," then felt a sudden stirring of uncertainty rising up. As he walked away, I called out, "I'm ten weeks pregnant!"

Not sure if he heard me, I watched as he crossed the room and spoke to a burly man with a long salt-and-pepper beard. As they conversed, Papa Joe glanced my way, his piercing blue eyes catching mine in a long stare. I was almost frightened, and if not for Margaret there with me, I might have run straight back to the car. I pulled my gaze away and searched for the exit just in case. His assistant came back to me, smiling, assuring me everything would be fine. He drew me over to the other side of the room where a massage table stood, and I lay down on my stomach. His assistant assured me that Papa Joe knew what to do. The burly man approached the table and without a word began to work on my feet with what appeared to be a hard crystal that he dug into my foot. Other times, he massaged my foot in a soothing, cyclical motion. I cringed a few times, uncertain what I was supposed to think or feel. At the end of my time with him, he said something to his assistant, who translated for me.

"Papa Joe would like to give you something," he said. He left for a few minutes, then came back with a handwritten note in English. As I waited outside for Margaret to finish her session, I unfolded the piece of paper.

"Heaven and the sounds of joy are close, especially for your honest desires. Keep emotions that negate what you want out of your expectations. Know that your chemical body is now balanced and the toxins are out. Keep to your intuition and not to the inhibitions. Within a very short moment, your answers are given. Just enjoy every moment until your baby is concepted." He signed it, "Blessings surround you."

I was blown away. How had he known I was afraid my body was toxic and that the pregnancy wouldn't last? I felt so relieved, and my "inhibitions" about my pregnancy were finally dispelled. When Margaret joined me after her session, both of us were so excited about what we had learned, but in reality, we had only been given a window into our own body's innate knowledge. I held on to Papa Joe's letter like a present, reading it often to confirm my secret wish would be fulfilled.

When the Maoris returned six months later, I went back once more to see Papa Joe. I was now eight months pregnant with my daughter. This time, I was encouraged to see him by my doula,

Anna, whom I had hired for my daughter's birth. In another serendipitous twist, she also worked with Papa Joe. She told me I should bring Owen. We walked into the house in Topanga, only this time, lines of women in various stages of pregnancy were waiting to see Papa Joe. I since learned that Papa Joe was known for helping women conceive, and as we walked closer, Papa Joe set eyes on Owen, the two of them locking each other's gaze for a moment. Owen was not even three years old. After their moment of connection, Papa Joe lifted his eyes to mine and beckoned me over. He didn't say a word as he reached for Owen's head, placing his hand on top of it, his other arm stretched out on a woman's belly as she lay on a mat. Owen seemed instinctively to know he was needed and therefore held still. Papa Joe closed his eyes as he connected Owen and the woman. I had no idea what was going on until Anna whispered in my ear.

"Maori healers believe that you are elevated by God when you have a child with Down syndrome. They see that child as a gift from God, a chosen one." I was riveted by the energy that was surrounding us, and when Papa Joe was done working with the woman on the mat, I hesitantly asked him what he thought about Owen.

His benevolent smile anchored me. "Owen is going to be Owen, and he will be fine. Do not worry about him." He motioned for me to step closer to him. He placed his hands on my burgeoning belly and felt for my baby's head. He slowly moved his hands around, inch by inch; incrementally, I felt the baby follow him as if seeking the energy of Papa Joe's hands. I had never felt something so incredible, so alive, so spiritual. I thanked him, and that was the last time I saw him.

I was so spiritually full in my life at that moment and so aware of how blessed I was. I felt time had begun to erase the negativity that had prevailed for so long in my mind. I was an active participant in a life that Owen was leading me through, drawing new people and experiences into my orbit that were beginning to replace the angst I had harbored for so long. Call it hormonal; call it growth. Either way, I was beginning to bloom from the inside out.

Chapter Seventeen

Two weeks before my due date, after a day of baking cookies, I finally found an interesting recipe: oatmeal chocolate chip with Grape-Nuts as the secret ingredient. They were crunchy and chewy, and in my nesting stage, I had baked dozens of them. Erik had a long-standing Monday night basketball game with guys he had known for years, so I headed to bed early as was my routine lately. The anticipation of the birth of my daughter helped, knowing each day brought me closer to my due date. I also was back to limping again because the baby was pressing on my sciatic nerve. Owen had done the same thing, putting me in misery during my final weeks of pregnancy. Later that night I was awakened by a strange scraping sound coming from the hallway. I looked over and Erik wasn't in bed. My nerves pinged as I slowly got up. The hallway light was on, and when I came out of the bedroom, I blinked. Erik was casually standing there, a chair in front of him.

"You woke me up," I said quietly in a cranky voice. He looked everywhere but at me.

"Why do you have the chair in the hallway?" I asked suspiciously. He mumbled something about needing to change the light bulb, and I frowned.

"Now? The light looks perfectly fine to me." It was then I noticed he was holding one leg up.

"What happened?" He looked down and tried to distract me yet again.

"What do you mean?" he asked, but he knew the gig was up.

"Okay . . . I hurt my ankle," he admitted. "But I'm sure it's just a little sprain. I'm fine, see?" He tried to let go of the chair and stand but fell back onto it heavily, wincing in pain. I was furious. Two weeks away from having a baby, and he'd injured himself.

"You do realize I am supposed to have our baby in two weeks? And I can't lift Owen up after my C-section? Who is supposed to take care of him?" I could feel my blood pressure rising. Anger suffused me. He tried to calm me, but it only made things worse. I stomped back to bed, not even offering to help him. He continued using the chair until he came to the bedroom.

"Hurts, doesn't it?" I asked caustically from the dark room.

He didn't answer for a moment as he tried to step on his foot gingerly. "I can't get to the bed," he said. "Can you help, please?"

I got up and put my arm around his waist. "I'm not happy about this, but I suppose I don't want to see you hurt yourself worse," I said, trying not to imagine an almost seven-foot man hop on one leg to get to bed.

"I promise I will be fine by the time the baby comes," he said meekly. I lay down, my head spinning. I couldn't sleep as I played forward the scenario of how I would manage the next two weeks with Erik injured. It felt so irresponsible of him to throw a wrench into my carefully laid plans. How much more could I take on, already nine months pregnant with a toddler? I was bone tired thinking about it. In the darkness, as his breathing lengthened into sleep, I tossed and turned. I wanted to chastise him for acting like a kid, trying to hide what he had done, knowing I was so close to the brass ring I was reaching for. I willed myself to back to sleep so I could put my rambling thoughts aside and deal with things in the morning, but a funny thing happened before morning came: I went into labor.

I woke up with a start, the night still black, and headed to the bathroom. I knew instantly that something had begun when my body started to cramp intermittently. Not wanting to turn the light on but feeling the need to look, there were already spots of blood. The kitchen light read five o'clock, and I stared at the calendar. Today was January 24, two weeks ahead of the date I had marked for my daughter's birth date. I called my doula, and she answered in a raspy, sleepy voice.

"Anna, I think I'm in labor," I whispered, not wanting to wake anyone in my house.

Silence.

"Anna?"

"You're two weeks away, and I'm in the middle of a birth right now," she said, a hint of hysteria edging her voice. She asked what symptoms I was having, and I told her. Somewhere deep inside me, I felt like I was wrong for not being able to control another birth, and I immediately heard myself apologizing for interrupting her.

"Maybe it was nothing."

"Call your doctor this morning, then call me back," she directed. We hung up and I went back to bed, hoping against hope I was wrong. I glanced over at Erik, and my stomach knotted again. What we were going to do?

That morning, I went to my doctor's office, and he seemed puzzled. "Your amniotic sac seems to be slowly leaking. But you aren't having any pronounced contractions."

"Then I'm not in labor? She's not coming now?" I asked, my mind again on the interruption of my carefully laid plans. Plus, there was my husband's injured foot to deal with.

"I think I'm going to admit you. We can't take a chance," he said. My eyes widened. I wasn't expecting to be admitted. I wasn't expecting this to happen. Not now, not yet, not when there was still so much to do! My mind briefly leapt back to the day I went into labor with Owen. I was two weeks early and unprepared. *This can't be happening again*, I thought. I mentally struck all items from my mind; every item on my to-do list would have to wait. I was going to the hospital. My bag was—barely—packed, but it would do. Cookies. *I'm so glad I baked my cookies for the staff*, flitted through my mind.

I called Erik, who informed me that his ankle was so bad he

may have broken it. I could hear his mom in the background. *Of course* he had called her to come and take care of Owen. She was always his backup, and whenever he called, she jumped into action. A part of me could hear her already. "What do you mean the baby's coming early? That's not the date you told me. Doesn't anyone adhere to rules these days? My babies . . ." Then she would retell her childbirth stories, claiming how easy it was for her.

I told Erik to find someone to bring my bag, and him, to the hospital. "Oh, and the cookies. Don't forget the cookies!" I said in a voice that bordered on admonishment, as if I were talking to a child. I felt like I was caught in a tornado of emotions. The anger from last night still lingered, while fear for the birth ahead began to rise within and was mixed with anticipation. But the most powerful emotion was a dizzying joy that I would soon meet my little girl.

In the maternity ward, I mulled over the irony of the situation, reminding myself that not once, but twice, my carefully laid plans had been thwarted in the birth of my child. I called Cynthia and asked if she wanted to come visit, as nothing appeared to be happening quickly. She brought magazines, candy, and snacks, even though I couldn't eat anything. In some weird, twisted way, it felt like a girls' slumber party. When visiting hours were over, she hugged me tight.

"I guess tomorrow I'll come back to meet the new little one," she said.

Then I got to work. I did everything I could to induce her arrival, walking the halls at intervals with the IV hooked up to my arm, breath work, and even squats when I could manage them. Night slowly faded into morning, and I had only managed a few hours of sleep. The staff woke me bright and early, puzzled that nothing had progressed. My doula popped in, but her lack of sleep was apparent too. And after consulting with my doctor, she told me she'd be back after she slept for a few hours.

The day progressed, but I didn't. I offered cookies to everyone who came to service me, and as the staff tried them, word got around that I was the "cookie mom." Meanwhile, Erik was off in another section of the hospital getting an X-ray on his foot, scooting around in a wheelchair. When he returned to the birthing room, he immediately began joking with the nurses and my doula, who had returned, and regaled them all with the story of how he injured himself. I was now in the beginning of the throes of hard labor, and he was winning them over, taking the attention away from me, from my beautiful birth story that was supposed to be unfolding exactly as I had planned. But yet again, it wasn't. My labor pains had increased with Pitocin, and every time I had a contraction, the pain was so severe I passed out. I all but screamed at Erik.

"Shut up," I said through gritted teeth. "I'm the one having a baby here. I need their attention. You don't!" His smile faded and he wheeled himself a little farther back. As he did, a nurse named Anna came into our room asking for him.

"Mr. Ostergard?" Anna said, holding a plastic bag.

"Yep, right here," he replied. She smiled sweetly at him, gently handing him the bag.

"I don't have your X-rays, but the Mexican food you ordered is here. Take good care of yourself!" Anna paused and looked at me empathetically. "Looks like a little one will be joining you soon. For your wife's sake, I hope your foot's not broken."

If I had any energy at that moment, I would have screamed, but I was depleted of any strength. As he opened the bag and the smell of Mexican food wafted my way, I almost threw up. With clenched teeth, I said to Anna, "If you don't tell him to throw that food out right now, I will divorce him as soon as the baby is born."

It took several more hours of intense labor before my doctor ordered a C-section. She breezed in, expecting that I would be dilated enough to push. Her smile wilted as she checked me.

"I don't know what's wrong, but something is definitely not right, because your cervix is swelling. I don't take chances when this happens. We're going to have to get you into surgery." After all this work, and pain, and trust in my body, I was shocked, and tears slid down my face as my doctor delivered the news.

Anna turned to me. "Listen. You and I both know you could have done this, but now your daughter is telling you something. Believe her. Trust her. She is telling you that a vaginal birth is not the safest way for her to arrive."

I thought having a VBAC (Vaginal Birth after Caesarian) would be a piece of cake, since I assumed Owen was born by C-section because of his diagnosis of Down syndrome. My disappointment was acute, but while the doctors performed the surgery, I heard an exclamation as the doctor stated, "Aha, there's the problem." Both assured me she was fine and healthy. After her birth, my doctor told me she had a true knot in the cord, which meant had I continued with a vaginal delivery, she may have been stillborn. My thanks to the doctor—and to my doula—for prevailing with calm when I realized that despite my best intentions to have a vaginal birth, they had averted another disaster in my world.

The X-rays on Erik's foot came back the next day; it was only a severe sprain. My default had been to pin the blame on him for going into labor early. Yet upon reflection, nothing would have changed the fact that my daughter was the one who alerted me that something was not right. She determined her birthday, not any circumstances surrounding it. This was just another reminder to let go and allow nature to lead. My grasp on control was slowly loosening.

Finally, I had the most beautiful, perfect sibling for my son. I felt like this time I'd gotten it right. I was holding a perfectly pink bundle of joy, who we named Tess. All the fanfare arrived. Flowers were delivered to my hospital room. Visitors showed up to meet her. Balloons decorated our house when we got home. Well-wishers sent gifts. My perfect baby moments were arriving, as was the reality of having two babies at home—not to mention an incapacitated husband for at least a few weeks. Regardless, I was on cloud nine because in my mind, this was a do-over, my chance to have the same experience almost every other parent had.

She was sleeping through the night within five weeks, eating well, and thriving. Because I had another C-section, my mobility was again compromised. But once she came home with us, we could relish in our little family of four. Owen didn't quite understand who this new creature was in our house; this tiny person who was now taking up the time I had reserved for him. I was breastfeeding her, which meant staying up late for her last feeding and getting up early.

Late one night, I sat in the den after feeding Tess, watching her exquisite features as she lay in my arms, overcome by slumber. I drank in her tiny features, her long fingers and toes, her button head. Then I heard a noise, a dragging sound. I gently got up to put Tess to bed, trying not to wake her, and almost stumbled over Owen, who was in the living room in his little footed blue pajamas, pacifier in his mouth. He sat there patiently, looking up at me with his soulful blue eyes.

"Owen, what are you doing?" I whispered. He stared at me. "I'll be right back." I put Tess in her crib and returned to him.

"Are you hungry?" He shook his head no. "What's wrong?"

He lifted his tiny arms to me, a gesture to pick him up. When I landed him in my arms, he snuggled his head into my chest and raised his hand, signing "I love you." He then signed "sleep." I wondered if Owen had come to keep me company—my little sentinel, standing guard in the night while I doted on this new little one. I had no idea if he had been up other nights, but somehow it would not have surprised me. I picked him up and brought him to his bed, lying down with him until he fell asleep.

Tentatively, as I walked into my new life with the two of them, I held my breath. I was afraid it would all be taken away. I feared losing what I had worked so hard for and gone through so much to achieve. I had not one, but two little ones, and each day brought a new wonder as they grew and thrived and—yes—fought. Owen now had the status of big brother in the family, and we treated him as such. Despite his constant therapies and revolving-door activities to help him achieve his milestones, he was also allowed to play with the baby, help feed her, and even take her diapers to the diaper pail. I always knew in my heart that the simplest way to raise a child to his potential was to treat him with potential. The best way I could do that was to start now by giving him small tasks, making him feel useful. Regardless of whether he had Down syndrome or not, I was not going to make that a reason why he couldn't do anything and everything.

Chapter Eighteen

When Owen was a baby, because of his diagnosis, there seemed to be a never-ending amount of paperwork that had to be filed with various doctors and state organizations, and every visit with a therapist required a signature. The first year was tinged with a bitterness when I sat with other moms and they talked about preschools, or baby swim classes, or tumbling classes. That's the paperwork I wanted to be filling out, vying for a spot in a preschool like the others. Despite my best attempts to feel part of their conversations, I felt like I was the lonely kid in high school who didn't fit in. I pretended to nod and smile while they discussed whether they should stop breastfeeding, or if it was too early for their child's first Happy Meal at McDonalds. My to-do listed looked like this: first therapist (then second, then third for PT and OT and play therapy), repeat blood test to check for aberrant cancer cells (kids with Down syndrome have a 25 percent greater chance of early childhood leukemia, but surprisingly, they react more favorably to treatment than typical kids), first eye exam to talk about the possibility of when (not if) he would need glasses, first extensive hearing exam to determine if he was born with any level of hearing loss, a follow-up heart sonogram, and every physical exam. Although parents of typical kids were subjecting their babies to some of the same tests, I didn't approach it from the 100 percent normal standpoint. I held my breath every time a doctor spoke with me. The medical condition somehow had to be documented, a baseline established, and protocol put in place. Only then did I look around and notice I was running to catch up to what typical moms were doing. I heard other moms talking about "Mommy and Me" classes and wondered how I missed that conversation. They mentioned new moms they'd met and play dates they had set up. While I was working in my own bubble of learning a new language of what it meant to have a child with Down syndrome, they were sliding into "best friends forever" play groups. I felt left out and left behind. I found nothing that fit the bill for my scenario: first-time mom, slightly frazzled, seeks Mommy and Me play group for kid with a disability, behind in milestones, willing to travel.

I asked other moms with kids older than mine for a few recommendations that led me to Sunnyside Mommy & Me, where I met with the director, Sarah, who eagerly welcomed Owen into her program.

Every Monday I showed up with Owen—I was the only working mom—and despite the mad dash as soon as class was over to drop Owen back home and get to the office, it was worth the hour of awkward yet conspiratorial meeting of moms. I was convinced I was the most socially insecure mom in the group, even though we were all bumbling through the initiation of first-time mom experiences. I had the kid with the disability. I assumed they were looking and judging and pointing mental fingers at Owen, covertly thinking, *See? That's why I took the test. That's what might have happened.* I pushed my self-consciousness aside and tentatively made a few friends. I was here and I was desperate, and that mindset won out against my nerves. I listened as they told their stories of loneliness or postpartum depression and thought, *Me too.* I understood that the ideal of the perfect day of "mommyhood" is sold to us in canned perfection just like everything else. It's marketed to make us feel like we can never be the perfect mom because she doesn't exist. But nevertheless, we all navigate our own choppy seas of this world called parenthood. I felt a bit of growth happen within me, a tiny seed of connection. We were all alike in our insecurities. On certain days mine were worse; other days they faltered.

I was still in the mode of explaining his diagnosis, but the other moms didn't care. They were newbies like me at this and just needed an outlet. We banded together in our shared dissolution of the perfect-mom dream. The class gave me the opportunity to insert my child into a group of typical kids and gave me my first taste of inclusion. For the other moms, it was their first taste of acceptance. I was giving myself permission to experience motherhood like others while experimenting with my own thought process of how I measured in comparison. So often I was envious, until I realized that perhaps they looked at me with envy for other aspects of my life that they didn't have: a thriving career and a husband at home who took care of our baby. Parenthood is such a steep learning curve, especially when we are forced to confront our insecurities instilled in childhood, which tend to show up in repetitive patterns. I was experiencing the rise of my own patterns. As a child, I preferred to disappear among the crowd, to retreat to my own space. Yet with Owen, I didn't have that luxury. He was, by his very nature, a standout, a child born with an extra chromosome, and that fact would always differentiate him from the crowd. The diversity in the group was also refreshing. There was the young mom who was married to a musician twenty years older than her. He traveled frequently, leaving her home to manage her son and process adulthood at the same time. She was beautiful and shy, and her painful admonition of the loneliness that surrounded her life made me wince. Another mom always appeared so put together—sporting a fashionable sundress every week with matching jewelry, makeup precisely applied, including lipstick—yet she belied the hunger in her to have another baby, which her husband said was out of the question. She pasted a smile on her face and shrugged it off. We all had our stories, our trials, and we found room to share without judgment, to give voice to our disappointments, our anger, and our hope—and sometimes even our sadness.

Yet I still had no reference point for my firstborn, no parents to ask questions and talk through issues with. I floundered when it came to simple things: What books should I read? What vitamins are suggested for children with Down syndrome? What kinds of therapy were others getting? What did milestones look like for other kids with Down syndrome?

When Owen was two, I was introduced to a woman who had a six-month-old daughter with Down syndrome. She had been the on the cover of the newsletter for Down Syndrome Los Angeles, and after a phone call with her, I studied her photo. She was a young and beautiful second grade teacher, and the photo of her with her daughter was angelic. This was the kind of person I wanted to meet. She was someone who I could identify with. She had a career, a life of hope before having a child with Down syndrome. She told me about another mom she met whose twins were the same age as her daughter, Ava. One of them had been diagnosed with Down syndrome. Impulsively, after a long conversation, I asked her to come over.

"Bring your friend," I said, so desperate was I to meet someone else in the same boat as me. We met one night, the three of us, and as soon as they arrived, there was no awkwardness, no niceties to get through. We had crossed an invisible line into a territory we were unfamiliar with but together in, and it sped up our intimacy. I offered a glass of wine, and we began a dense conversation of our lives up until now. I felt an internal release and a sense of relief as we spoke. None of us would have met had it not been for the diagnosis. We never had any reason to cross paths, living in a city like Los Angeles. Yet here we were, a seed of friendship sprouting from our fragility. That night, we agreed meeting on a regular basis should be the next step, and we would put the word out in case there were other like-minded moms. They both seemed reticent to be the genesis of the group, probably because we all felt so overwhelmed.

"Girls, this is what I do. I plan things. I make events happen. I'll host once a month. And even if nobody but us show up, it guarantees that I get to keep our conversation going." They nodded, still unsure what they had committed to. I had never felt more right about something in my life. I couldn't take Owen's diagnosis away, and I couldn't let the feeling I got from this meeting dissipate. Our gathering had generated such a sense of belonging, and I wasn't going to let it slip away. I appreciated my group of moms with typical kids, and I needed them, but this group addressed the hunger for identification, which had been awoken, and I couldn't ignore. I needed to find my own tribe, not hover on the edge of the new parents' circle where I felt like an intruder at times—unidentifiable, the box marked "other."

The next month, anticipating just the two of them, eight women showed up at my door bearing wine and a dish to share. We were women in all stages of life, ranging from early twenties to mid-forties. Some of us were full-time moms, some were working moms, some had more kids than just their child with Down syndrome. Each week, new friendships were formed within our group, brought together by the common denominator of an extra chromosome—as if that extra chromosome somehow glued us together by an invisible connection. I looked around my living room at the beautiful women who were connecting: talking, laughing, and crying. I felt tears sting my eyes as I thought, *What incredibly cool women I have surrounded myself with.* The stereotype of the frumpy, middle-aged woman having a child with Down syndrome was swept out of my mind as we all shared our stories through tears and laughter.

Each month, without fail, I would send out a reminder about the "Moms Group," adding more and more email addresses. My brain cells were stuck on autopilot. Even the writer in me couldn't figure out a better title to this group of dynamic women. Eventually, it became a secret acronym to me—"MOMS: Mentoring Other Moms"—because at the heart of it, that's what we were doing. I didn't need to quantify it by adding "extra" or "special." We were simply a group of moms hungry for connection. We told friends, and friends of friends, and women emailed me and called me who I had never met, asking if they could join our group. I looked forward to that gathering every month, and when I became pregnant with my third child, other moms jumped in to host it, enabling us to reach out further and further into our community. This was the days before Evite, Mailchimp, and GroupMe apps, so I painstakingly collected emails in a folder and typed them in each month, watching my list grow and grow. With every new recruit, I would conspiratorially write, "It's the coolest club you never wanted to join."

We met in Hollywood, Pasadena, and Santa Clarita, even meeting as far as the South Bay and Manhattan Beach. Our meetings were a place to gather and find a friendly smile, or a chance to cry and maybe regain the hope we all needed so desperately. Our families grew as well, and we welcomed new babies and siblings for our children. One mom organized a pumpkin patch get-together, and another mom had a pool party. Sometimes it was a park day or a birthday party or a beach day. When those events came up, we showed up, but not because we had to; we showed up because we needed to. We wanted our kids to see others who had Down syndrome, to meet them and play with them, to forge their own bonds as they grew. We needed each other as moms to ask about milestones and trade doctor recommendations and therapies. We needed our husbands to meet so they could see who we spent our time with as we all blocked out that once-a-month Wednesday. We felt safe, included, and even special in a world where our children were considered "less than."

We retreated to this club to talk about the sadness, the guilt, the tests we took or didn't take. We shared our birth stories, and sometimes our horror stories, when doctors mistreated us because we were the anomaly; we were the statistic they didn't want to have on their record.

One night, as a group of us sat on the floor of the living room, wine glasses in hand, we talked of our desire to have a celebrity, any celebrity, who could identify with us. With a hint of truth, we suspected that celebrities would never entertain carrying to full term a pregnancy with a child who was diagnosed with Down syndrome. "Imagine the horror," we'd said. "Imagine the paparazzi following them around, challenging them on their decision. Imagine the blow to their celebrity-ness." Imagine. Just imagine. Then one mom chimed in. "I mean, we just need Julia Roberts to have a kid with Down syndrome, then everyone will think it's super cool." We laughed, and another mom, said, "What about Brangelina? Could you imagine how sexy Brad Pitt would make it seem to have a child like ours?" As we threw out celebrity names, the laughter became more raucous until tears ran down my face. Imagine. Just imagine.

A mom showed up at one of our Wednesday night gatherings, hugely pregnant with her second baby who was just given a diagnosis of Down syndrome. She was beautiful in the way only pregnancy can make you glow. Her auburn hair was thick and shiny, and she radiated life. I introduced myself to her, and she told me she was eight months pregnant with a little boy. She had an older son who was typical, and I wistfully thought of how she had the best experience first: a typical son who hit all his milestones and was perfect from the moment he was born. Her second pregnancy was a red alert, a fire alarm, so they took the test for Down syndrome and it came back positive. She poured her story out to me and told me how her doctor refused to manage her pregnancy as she started her eighth month of pregnancy. His words were like salt on an open wound.

"He thought I should have done something different," she told me, implying that "different" meant "termination." She left his office, feeling unbelievably hurt and betrayed by the medical community. She found our group through a friend, and it was a night for her to pour out her heart and her tears to the women who understood. We had all suffered a bias against our children at one point or another. People can be insensitive, at best, when it comes to something they don't know or have been programmed to be afraid of. I often wonder why the medical community has banded together to make us feel so afraid of a child with Down syndrome, as if it is a foreign alien growing inside of us. Why project that it's the worst diagnosis you can ever get, when this diagnosis can't be defined merely by its traits? My child is not like the next child, or the next, and in hindsight, I wouldn't wish away one minute of the life I have lived with my Owen.

Those Wednesday nights with my tribe of women became a solace for me during the years when Owen was a toddler. The conversations weren't always so heart-wrenching. We laughed a lot as we discovered that we all shared the same intense love for our kids, a ferocious kind of love that resonated in our deepest core.

We had given birth to the most vulnerable of humans, yet we would come to learn they were the actually most resilient—alert and alive to life in ways a typical human can never be. There is something about the loving, kind creatures that our children are that puts them in a bracket with a far greater impact on humanity, yet it is invisible in its human form.

When the National Down Syndrome Conference came to Southern California, Owen was two years old. Another parent asked me to help staff a booth for a nonprofit working on a treatment for kids with Down syndrome that would elevate their cognitive level. He mentioned the scientists would be at the booth as well. I was intrigued. I had not bothered to read any scientific research after I spent too much time looking up the worst outcomes of Down syndrome, so I was unaware of what future advances were being addressed. This was different, though, because I had access to credible doctors and scientists, doctors who had labs where they studied mice bred with the extra chromosome that led to Down syndrome. They were actively pursuing research that could help me understand my child.

When we arrived, I was introduced to Dr. Mobley, who was working with Down Syndrome Research and Treatment Foundation (now LuMind IDSC), an organization I had not heard of. He told me about his research at UC San Diego, where he was breeding mice with the genetic makeup of Down syndrome in order to create a treatment that would raise their cognitive ability by a few percent.

"This could make a difference in the quality of life for some kids," he said.

"What does that mean exactly?" Without waiting, I peppered him with more questions. "Does it mean my son will go to college? Will he get married?"

Dr. Mobley looked at me with a smile on his face. "I plan to dance at your son's wedding, that's how confident I am in what we are discovering." Those were the kinds of words I was looking for, the assuredness I wanted and needed. I saw a way out of what I perceived to be a life of suffering. I didn't need to comb through scientific journals to read how genetic mutations made my son what he is. I wanted validation of the kind of person Owen would be with this particular genetic makeup. Would he be kind? Would he be funny? Would he talk? Sing? Dance? Would he be sad sometimes? Genetics can show a picture, but they can't write the story of who a person will be. I wanted to hear what might be possible for my son so I could dream bigger than what the textbooks said he would be or do. I had read and heard all the stories of what he might never be able to do, but nobody had expressed that there could be more, so much more, and now I was beginning to form my own hypothesis of a better life for my son.

I was infused with a new hope. Immediately after the convention, I dove into fundraising for the organization. I addressed our mom's group, soliciting volunteers. I explained, with all the fervor of an ardent activist, what their research hoped to do. I wanted something to reach for. I needed something to finally push me out of the sense of hopelessness that had guided me until then. I formed a team of moms from the group to help me, and we secured a donated venue. We didn't make much on that first event, but what we did gain was attention. The crowd of parents, therapists, doctors, and friends were fascinated with the research and the possibilities. Out of that grew our annual fundraiser for DSRTF. We spent months planning, holding nightly sessions at my house full of wine and laughter. Not only did I have a group of moms who grew out of a unique connection; this group was willing to dive in deeper, to give more time and energy to help me build a new vision for our kids' future. Places like the Hollywood Bowl and ritzy hotels in LA became our playground for a night with all those we had met and who had supported us along the way. Like a snowball rolling down the mountain, I cheered as we gained an avalanche of support from every corner of our lives. Those who heard my story never questioned; they only asked where to sign up. Of course, it helped to have my little man, my Owen, as a living, breathing motivation.

In the end, I moved on from the fundraisers but never forgot the friendships, the loyalty, and the bonds that were formed over one extra chromosome. It started as a celebration of hope for my child but became a platform that helped me hone in on the everyday spirit our kids are born with—the individual charismatic personalities that shone in our daily lives.

Over time, I came to understand that by fueling my life with meaningful action, not just the empty promise of hope, I was able to watch my son's unique personality and brilliance emerge. Maybe society doesn't often see that brilliance because it comes in bits and pieces. But I know the secret. I know what hides beneath is a deep well of love and affection that completes me.

When I was in my teens, growing and stretching into adulthood, I often hid away in my room, reading and writing and pondering what my life would be like when I left the shackles of childhood. I imagined I was going to do something big and that I was destined for greatness—as we all think at one time or another. I had no context for what that would be. But I knew in my heart that somehow, someday, I would have my moment of glory. Perhaps my son was the context, the impetus, for stepping into my greatness. Perhaps this yearning to find something bigger than myself was presented to me in the rare present that was my son. Perhaps the lesson was about rising to the occasion, finding the quiet greatness within ourselves, and doing what needed to be done.

Chapter Nineteen

For two years straight, Eva called almost daily.

"What is Owen doing now?" she asked, her voice a cheery question. I enthused about the most recent milestone he had reached. The night before, when I played a set of miniature bongos for him, he finally rose onto all fours and crawled toward me, a gleeful smile on his face. My voice was filled with pride as I told her.

"His cousin has been doing that for months." Her dismissal of Owen's ability to do anything noteworthy fed into my own criticism of him, and I silently urged him to do something, anything, before a typical kid.

When he was a year and a half, Owen managed to climb the stairs on a slide and go down on his own despite not being able to walk yet, and his therapist cheered.

"That's a two-and-a-half to three-year-old skill," she said. Feeling confident I could share that with Eva, I told her, waiting for a positive response.

"Is that on a Down syndrome chart?"

"No, that's on a typical chart."

"Well, that's ridiculous, because his cousin has been doing that for months, and they are the same age," she retorted.

My victory had become a defeat yet again with just one comment. I had such a hard time with her insistence that he would never amount to much. Her inference that he was broken from the start informed how she treated him.

Yet despite her resistance to him, she couldn't keep away from him. She offered to babysit and often kept him overnight if we wanted to go out. She even watched him for a long weekend while Erik and I went to New York. I shook my head at times, perplexed by her dual personality, which made it so confusing when I didn't know who would show up. Some days, I watched her from afar as she cuddled him, sang to him, and kissed him. I almost imagined that she loved him more than we did, that she somehow felt she was his champion. And for that reason, she had to test her own belief system and the reality against our hopes and dreams for him. She never talked about her childhood; maybe her own life reflected disappointments that translated into her feelings about Owen.

Walking was the one milestone I anticipated the most, the brass ring I was hoping to catch. If Owen could just walk within the typical age range, then I could own that triumph and finally lay to rest the fears that he would fall so far behind other kids and never catch up.

I came home every day and asked Erik the same thing: "Anything yet?" I had seen so many babies go from walking to crawling within a few weeks to a few months, and I was ready for it. Of course, well-meaning friends told me, "You don't want them to walk. It's so much more work!" I was suffused with envy as I watched them follow their child around, not realizing how much it hurt to hear. I would have given anything for my child to start walking on a typical child's timeline; instead, I was sidelined with him as they chatted together while their toddlers toddled. My son sat there, blissfully content to be wherever he was at.

Yet I kept reading and researching and eventually had an idea. If he couldn't walk, why not work on other things he might be able to accomplish while we were patiently waiting? I wanted a "golden child" too—a milestone that surprised everyone. I needed a win.

Just once, I wanted to silence Eva in her comparisons. I had no idea if it would work.

A random post in a Down syndrome chat group about potty-training caught my eye. A mom had taught her daughter to use the toilet when she was only one year old. I read it again and then consulted the normal timeline for kids with Down syndrome. According to the books I had on hand, some didn't become potty-trained until five or six years old, and others continued to wear diapers even longer. The mental picture that inserted itself into my mind when I thought of my son wearing diapers at age five or older didn't fit with any timeline I had prepared for. And I would never be able to handle Eva's disdain.

The following weekend, I went to Target and bought a child's toilet seat. When I walked in the door, Erik looked at me lugging the box, a question forming in his eyes.

"I know, I know! You think he's too young. But he's not. I read this woman's post . . . We are going to teach him to use the toilet."

"When?" Erik asked.

"Now," I said. "Today. I know he's not even two years old, but there's no reason we can't try."

"Can I ask why?" he said, implying that he knew we were going forward with the plan, regardless of any input from him.

"I have a theory. Maybe if we teach him Owen sit on the toilet, he will learn to anticipate the physicality of needing to go pee. Then he will be potty-trained sooner rather than later." I unboxed the toilet seat, and he followed me as I set it in the corner of the bathroom.

"Books. We need books." I retrieved a few and set them next to the toilet seat. "Now, whenever either of us has to go, we bring Owen into the bathroom and put him on the toilet seat. Give him a book if you have to."

He raised his hand, and I smiled.

"Yes?"

"How will he tell us if he has to go? He can't talk yet."

"Easy. He can sign the word for potty."

I showed him. Owen was already quite prolific in sign language, with over thirty words that he used to communicate. I walked over to Owen and picked him up, showing him the word for potty. Erik followed me as I sat him down on the seat in the bathroom. He smiled and repeated the sign for potty. Then, to our astonishment, we heard him tinkle.

"Okay, that's a fluke. It probably won't happen like that all the time," I said, secretly pleased.

I squatted down in front of Owen. "Good job! Potty!" I signed the word again.

A few hours later we repeated the task, and he went again, his little hand waving the sign. The rest of the day I watched Owen closely, and every few hours, like clockwork, he raised his little hand, signed, and I rushed him into the bathroom. Perhaps he thought it was a game, but in my heart, I wanted to believe that this was my brilliant little boy, sending me a signal that he was smart, that I could count on him to rise up to the challenge. The next few days we watched in amazement as he signaled to us every time he needed to go. Before bedtime, we put him in a diaper, and he woke up dry. Erik and I were beginning to feel like we had won the lottery, and I joked that our toddler couldn't toddle yet, but he sure could use the toilet. I finally had bragging rights.

Then came my favorite moment. Eva called.

"What's this I hear? Owen is potty-trained? I can't believe it."

"It's true. It happened overnight."

I basked in the prolonged silence.

"Kids can't do that, Suzanne. Through the night too? Ridiculous. I'm sure he's holding it in, and it's going to become an issue. You should probably let your doctor know."

I could feel my cheeks burn. Why can't my son do something for once without her disputing it?

"Other parents have done it too. It's not an issue. Maybe this is a sign that he's smart." There, I'd said it. My kid can be smart too. I could hear Eva's judgmental laughter.

"Smart? He has Down syndrome. Your kid isn't going to be smart. Now his cousin, he's smart."

I rolled my eyes, silently suffering as she went on. I told Erik to prove it to her by inviting her over so she could see for herself.

"When I'm not home," I said pointedly.

My faith in Owen was empowering. It was the spark I needed to begin my own transformation from mourning the child I thought I was going to have to celebrating the child who was emerging. His tics and behaviors and glorious milestones were all smashed into one little person whose personality could love harder than anyone I knew.

I could engage in my life again as I slowly, tentatively emerged from the cocoon I had built around me. Like the butterfly, I had found the transformation painful but necessary. I had turned a corner in the processing of my mental spirit, drawing now upon a greater source of strength as I watched Owen expand while his baby sister—effortlessly, it seemed—reached the same milestones in less time.

But I still had setbacks as my journey curved and veered off track on occasion. Some days I felt like I had vanquished the niggly doubts that plagued me, the errant whispers of my mind when I would see my son act differently than a typical child. He had a way of putting one hand on each side of his face, wide open like jazz hands, and his body would shake as he tightened all the features on his face. "Stimming," the therapists called it. It bothered me, and if anyone saw him do it, I would apologize. I would make excuses for him. It was a quirk of his, and I couldn't quite figure out why he did it. Was he excited? Nervous? Afraid? More importantly, I had to turn inward and ask myself, *Why does Owen's behavior bother me?* Was it because of the looks we'd get from others? Was it because other kids would sometimes come up to me and say, in their blunt way, "Why does he do that?" I wondered why he did certain things too.

The kids always preferred that their dad took them to the park, and I preferred it that way as well. My childhood home in Michigan was on an acre of land with a river running through the back of it. There were plenty of kids in our family to play an impromptu whiffle ball game or hide-and-seek. But Erik had grown up in Los Angeles, and taking him and his brother to the park was part of the daily ritual. He was also tall, which allowed him to hoist the kids to the top of the monkey bars, or follow them down the slide. He was gentle and powerful at the same time. He boosted their confidence, not their fears—as I was wont to do—by the way he allowed them to explore and progress. But on the occasional weekend when I felt motivated to take them, I suited up with my best let's-go-to-the-park attitude, strapped them into the stroller, and walked over.

Saturdays were always busy, so I tried to go in the late afternoon when parents were packing up blankets and snacks and chairs, hoisting toddlers in their arms, and dashing away as fast as they could before the meltdowns began. One Saturday, when Owen was about three years old, I headed to the park with Tess asleep in the stroller. I staked out my territory, choosing a corner as far away as I could get from other parents having a playdate meetup and surreptitiously looked around to see if anyone I knew was there. I sat Owen down in the sand, to the side of the biggest slide. A handful of parents were several feet away on the other side, lost in conversation with each other. Kids and parents began to desert the area, heading to their cars. I took his shoes off and he sat contentedly, sifting sand through his toes while I placed a few toys within reach. Glancing up, I saw two boys who were about six years old at the top of the slide. They looked at Owen, pointing and taunting him.

"Freak!" one boy called out, then turned to look at his friend and giggled.

"Freak boy!" the boy's friend mimicked, pointing and glancing at his friend, the two finding a camaraderie in their little game.

I was furious, even though I had anticipated a moment like this. I had been waiting for someone to call out his distinctive characteristics of Down syndrome, his upward-slanted eyes and flattened facial features, and now he was doing that thing with his hands again. Being at the park stimulated him, which is why he did it, I assumed. I just hadn't expected two boys to boil it all down to the word *freak*. I walked slowly over to the slide.

"What did you say?" They looked at me a little daunted.

"He's a freak," one of them said again, not nearly as confident.

I was looking around for their parents but couldn't see anyone close by. In an instant, a rage bubbled inside me, and I couldn't help myself as I gritted my teeth and spoke, slowly drawing the words out.

"Is that what you think? Well, you're ugly. Did your parents tell you that? Maybe they should have before you started calling other little boys names."

I could feel the words slipping out before I could catch them, and the two boys looked at me and dashed off. It was not my proudest moment, and I cringed to think that those little boys thought my son was a freak. If I couldn't protect Owen from the barbs of boys at three years old, how could I protect him as he grew up?

I began packing up the sand toys, my hands still shaking. "Come on, buddy, let's go home." I needed a big glass of wine after that, and a spiritual reckoning.

I didn't tell anyone what happened at first, and it wasn't until the moms gathered again that I spilled the story, prefacing my reaction with my inability to stop myself from the words that tumbled out. There's always one mom, usually a teacher, who advises that I should have seen it as a "teaching moment" and taken my time to explain to the boys about my son's diagnosis. Another mom exploded with laughter.

"Are you kidding me? Who has time to think of the right words to say? You said what you thought, and it's the parents' fault for not raising better boys."

Both were right, in their own way, but perhaps the moment was not a teaching moment for the boys, but for me. I had confronted the bully, so to speak, the haunting of a moment that I knew would come to pass. I was actively learning. I was being taught by both typical kids and by my son that we could all teach and be taught. The boys had taught me to stand up for my son, but I also knew that my response had been childish. I could have given them a helpful message, or at least acted less retaliatory. Life lessons were all around me, waiting to be unpacked.

Chapter Twenty

From the day of my son's diagnosis, when I thought I would never get through the milestones, suddenly time seemed to be racing by. Despite those first dark days when moments stretched forever as our family wrestled with the diagnosis, we now seemed to move into a gentler stretch of time. Tess brought a normalcy to the equation as we transitioned into the two-child phase, and with it came an ease of parenting as school loomed on the horizon for Owen.

We visited a few schools and found what was then called a "preschool mix," which was a class consisting of fifteen typical kids and five special needs kids. The idea was that blending a few special needs kids in with typical kids would help both groups; seeing their peers master milestones would help the kids with special needs, and the other kids learned to accept them as part of their setting. The school was quite far from our house, and the first few days Owen cried when we dropped him off.

"Don't worry," the teacher assured me. "They all cry at first. He'll stop in a few minutes after you're gone."

I left my heart in that classroom with him as I forced myself to turn away and leave him. The class seemed wildly chaotic to me, but day after day, I came to realize these kids were just being kids:

rambunctious, playful, and loud. I looked around to see if I could identify the other kids with a disability, but they all blended in so well together. It was a class helmed by two women named Ms. Close and Ms. Pat, who had been teaching together for over thirty-five years. I liked them immediately. Ms. Pat always talked loudly because, she explained, "I'm deaf in one ear, so I understand the kids who have disabilities."

The hours Owen was in school gave me a chance to bond with Tess. I had dropped to part-time at my job, feeling the pull of motherhood and watching time slip by dangerously fast. Each day when it was time to pick Owen up, I waited outside the fence with the other parents, looking for my little man in his glasses to come out in the tumble of kids who surged toward the gate. He never charged out. Instead, he was always bringing up the rear as the teachers urged him to pick up the pace. That was one thing about Owen that never changed and never would: he moved in his own time, his stride often lagging behind others. In my rush to always be moving faster and jumping ahead, Owen is the one who forced me to slow down and exercise patience.

His teachers and I spent a few minutes talking. They appreciated the chance to connect with me and my willingness to understand Owen's learning progress. I was the mom who asked questions, who dug for answers, who established a connection with his teachers because they were now a vital part of his day. After months of fence-side chats, they finally conceded that Owen had cried for an hour the first day and then continued to cry every day that week. By then, my resolve was greater, and I knew what I was doing was for his greater good.

One day, late to pick him up, I came to the gate and saw the teachers with Owen next to a big yellow school bus. Owen climbed down the steps, chatting away in his almost legible language, waving goodbye to the bus driver.

Ms. Pat came over to me. "He's really interested in the bus. I think you should consider putting him on it. It would give him more independence," she said.

I looked at her with fear clutching my heart. "Really? The bus? I mean . . . I can do that if you think it would help," I stuttered.

The bus looked so incredibly big and long for my little man to get into.

She nodded. "I wouldn't tell you to do it if I didn't think he was ready."

That day, I came home and called the school district and asked for bus transportation. Within a week, a big yellow bus pulled up to our house an hour before school started. I went outside with Owen and introduced myself to the bus driver.

"It takes an hour to get him to the school?" I asked.

She nodded. "I have other kids to pick up, so it really depends on that. Don't worry, he'll be fine."

She showed Owen to a seat, and I watched as she pulled out a jerry-rigged seatbelt that looked like a full-body harness.

"What is that?" I asked.

"His seatbelt. We have to put him in the harness until we can trust that he won't take his seat belt off."

I looked at her, and doubt settled into the pit of my stomach. "Why can't you trust him first? Then, if he doesn't keep the lap belt on, you can put him in this." It resembled a straightjacket, and I felt as if it was too confining. I held my ground, and the bus driver acquiesced. I'm sure these rules were put in place for a reason, but I wasn't going to send my kid to school in a straightjacket, especially at three years old. I backed off the bus, waving goodbye to Owen. His lower lip started to quiver, and I waved at him with a big smile, willing him to be good, to be happy. Willing him to not cry.

The bus lurched down the street as I watched him disappear, his glasses perched on his nose, the slight turn of his head to see me until he was gone. As soon as the bus left, Erik's car turned the corner. We had planned ahead that Erik would follow the bus because . . . well, we were new parents who had just sent our tiny baby boy off on a big yellow school bus with someone we didn't know.

An hour later, Erik arrived home. "It was fine. The driver was cautious. But it seems like a long time for him to sit on a bus to get to school." We both calmed ourselves by remembering that we could always cancel the bus. It really did seem to give him a bit more independence. Sometimes, though, when the bus was late bringing him home, I felt a twinge of fear that something bad had happened. On the last day of preschool when Owen graduated, his teachers again confessed to me.

"We suggested the bus but didn't realize you would take us seriously."

Because I had come to like and respect them over the past two years, we laughed about it. "Really? I thought all the other parents were doing the same thing!"

"No, you were the only one who said yes!" Pat yelled, given that she couldn't hear herself. It turns out I would always be the parent to say yes, assuming everyone had my son's best interest in mind. But as we continued the education journey, I came to realize that wouldn't always be the case, and I forced myself to listen more intently to the advice given.

In the meantime, I was shuttling Tess to a small preschool around the corner named The Magic Yard, aptly named for a place where a tire swing hung from an overgrown avocado tree, and a pirate ship anchored itself in the sandbox. The entire day was spent finding nooks and crannies to play together in a surreal, enchanted yard. Because of Owen's traditional school setting, it took me a while to realize that school was play, and parents wanted to connect, to set up play dates outside of preschool. I was caught off guard by the fact that I didn't have to "explain" anything about my daughter, and we suddenly were on invite lists for birthday parties and play dates, something I hadn't experienced as easily with Owen. It was such a novelty to me, this typical world of parenting and preschool, where women I noticed and admired paused to start a conversation and initiate a friendship.

As we rounded the corner to kindergarten, I looked for any sign from the universe to ensure I was making the right choice for my child. Everything felt wrong, though, and I had not yet learned how to rely on my instincts. Instead, I relied on outside sources, specialists who told me what they thought of my child, whom they barely knew.

Our choices were limited to what the school district would offer. Given three choices of special day classes (SDC), we visited all of them, and with each progressive classroom, I felt defeat creep in. I wanted to be able to enroll him in the local school, like every other kid, but the institutions that were defining my son's educational road were pointing me in another direction because of his disability. We crisscrossed the city, driving from one school to another, hoping the next one would offer the right placement. What was I hoping for? Even I couldn't define that. I felt like we were just another case number, that Owen was just another kid who had to be inserted into the system and classified by his disability.

I had the sinking feeling that I didn't have a choice. I had to choose the "best of" what lay before me. We settled on a school in North Hollywood that enrolled a smaller number of kids. Owen was the only child with a diagnosis of Down syndrome. We did our due diligence. Owen was tested so he could be determined MR (mentally retarded), words I cringed at every time I saw them on his paperwork. Later, they would change the terminology from MR to ID (intellectual disability), but it still crushed me when I saw his MR designation on all his early records. His file grew bigger year by year. The IEP (Individualized Education Plan) was the bible that the educational staff would live by throughout the school year.

His classroom was segregated from the general population of the school, literally sectioned off by a fence, although we were told that they would be integrated as they matured. All these new phrases I had to learn: mainstream, preschool mix, IEP, mild-to-moderate, moderate-to-severe—not to mention the services that would be attached to them. Occupational therapy (OT), physical therapy (PT), speech therapy. But the word I didn't pay enough attention to in the beginning was *inclusion*, as I went along with the tide that was pulling me in the direction of special education. Owen was my oldest, so I had no idea what an inclusion model looked like, and to be honest, the district never shared that model. Whether they didn't want to or were instructed not to, I would never know.

Kindergarten seemed like it was working, as far as we knew, and the reports always came back stating, "What a wonderful boy," or "He's so funny!" It wasn't until Owen had spent the better part of two years in the class that I realized he hadn't learned to read, and he often played jokes on the teachers and hid under the desks when he didn't want to be on task. I found a recurring theme that became visible to me: attend to the child most in need, then address the others. It's a slogan they use on the airlines if your plane loses oxygen: put on your mask first, then your child's mask. But that's for life-threatening situations; this was occurring daily for my child. By the time Owen was in first grade, I was starting to look for answers. Why wasn't he learning to read? Every typical child around us was reading Early Reader books. It was at this point I started to question the model he was in. What was really going on in the classroom? I was alerted to new habits he would come home with, such as rolling around on the floor, or interrupting us by singing loudly, or fixating on toys or objects that he had never shown an interest in before. Oh, and he had begun biting other kids.

Chapter Twenty-One

At the ten-week mark of pregnancy with my third child, I panicked. What am I doing? How can I disturb this wonderful family Erik and I have built with yet another baby? Can I trust myself enough to know that everything will be okay? I was fully invested in creating a life for Owen that would challenge the textbook diagnosis and in carving out a place for him in our world—not a special needs world. And I was inherently enjoying the ease with which Tess was exploring her world and progressing. The two loved each other and were constant companions.

So here I was, forty years old and, ironically, with a higher risk than ever of having a child with Down syndrome. I made an appointment with a new doctor, who would be the third doctor to deliver my third child, given that my insurance had changed yet again. With Tess's birth I was adamant that I wanted to try for a VBAC (vaginal birth after caesarean), so I switched doctors. Once again, my unborn child and I were interviewing a new doctor. His office was busy, which I took as a good sign.

I waited for the doctor and thought about the answers to the questions he would ask. I was no longer the first-time mom, arrogantly pregnant, or the mom desperate to right the wrong and have a typical child. I was now confident enough in my ability to know where I stood in my thought process while also having an awareness that no pregnancy is without some trepidation, some doubt that a complication could arise. I had pleaded with Erik that we try for a third—actually, I insisted. At the same time, I wondered how this new life would impact our family, the world that I had so carefully cultivated and so neatly organized. We were happy together; would I have more room to love another? There was no turning back now, though, as the door slowly opened and the doctor came in. He introduced himself and looked at my chart.

"Before you say anything," I began wearily, "I already know that I am what you call 'advanced maternal age.' I am your statistic. I already have a child with Down syndrome who is five years old. I know my odds, and I don't have any plans to test with this baby." He smiled slowly. I was prepared for pushback, but I wasn't prepared for what he said next.

"Thank you for telling me. I appreciate your honesty. I have a grandson who was born with William's syndrome, and he's four years old now. He is a blessing and a gift from God."

His eyes twinkled as he said what I wanted to hear next. "Let's have a baby!"

As the words sunk in, I knew that the universe was on my side. This moment, this beautiful acknowledgement that my life was on course, settled within me. Someone once told me that when you are pregnant, your child leaves a message in the womb, inscribed for the next baby. Perhaps Owen made Tess aware that I needed her to color in the spaces of my life that felt damaged; to reform my idea of perfection. Her presence helped me understand that perfection comes in all shapes and forms. With my youngest, whatever message Owen and Tess may have left for him, his peaceful and sweet demeanor brought an added element of wonder to our lives. I not only expanded my love with his addition to our family, but I watched as he effortlessly rounded out the corners of our family of four and cemented our definition as a tribe of five.

On the eve of Axel's birth, which was scheduled given that the last two had resulted in C-sections, I couldn't sleep. I woke in the early hours and pondered what life would be like with three kids. I wanted this birth to go smoothly, but as with all life events (and major surgery), there was no guarantee. I prayed, contemplating my journey that had brought me to the cusp of the birth of my third child. I had traveled my own mountains of adversity, unraveled my deepest fears, and examined them. My journey with Owen and Tess had each woven a strength into my new parenting armor, a determination to discover what path was my mine to trod, strewn with challenges and triumphs. I was rewarded with the ease of pregnancy and birth when Axel entered my world. His name was a relic of Erik's heritage, his great-grandfather's name, and meant "father of peace."

People asked me on occasion, "How do you manage?" and I almost didn't understand the question. The early days when my kids were ages one, three, and five years old, I didn't think about how I did it, I just did what had to be done. I spent so much of Owen's babyhood wishing things were different and trying so many new things to combat the diagnosis that having two more typical kids was like learning how to sail. Once you know how, it's all about the joy in the ride. Yet I was very conscious of what it took for me to acquire that freedom of a new, expansive world. I watched in awe every day as the younger ones learned to do things without therapists and prompts. Taking the kids out with me was like a marathon. I prepared for it and made sure none of my needs had to be addressed. To be honest, I liked the physical endurance: pick one kid up, put one down, unload the double stroller, catch one kid as he walked in the wrong direction. I was in control and proud of my little tribe. It's no accident that moms with young kids have great biceps; they are like iron weights, picking them up and down all day long.

It didn't take long for Axel to realize that he was smarter than Owen. As he grew, I began to think of him as the "big little brother" when he would stand on his three-year-old legs like a tiny version of Mighty Man and hold on tight to Owen's arm, yelling, "Mommy, Owen's running away!"

Like any other mom, I kept doing what had to be done. The extra layer of Down syndrome was work, yes, but perhaps it taught me how to handle my typical kids more easily. Maybe there was an order to it all that I couldn't yet see, but others did. I had a friend with two boys, and after I had Axel, she got pregnant with a third. I was surprised, since she indicated that she wasn't going to have any more.

"I was done having kids," she told me. "But you made it look so easy."

Chapter Twenty-Two

By the spring of Owen's first grade year, I knew I wanted to transition him to inclusion, which meant having a different conversation with the district—one they didn't necessarily like. I could tell by the way they never spoke of it, never offered it as a solution, and were quick to take it off the table when he was younger. Was I prepared for it? The simple answer was always no, but Erik always said yes. I had been told by other parents that inclusion would be a fight, and I must be prepared to "lawyer up." Erik firmly believed we would get whatever we wanted; it was just a matter of how we steered the conversation.

Meeting day came and, as usual, I brought fruit and muffins, my practical way to break the awkward silence. Coached by others that food was like offering an olive branch, it had helped on previous occasions, but this meeting started out tense, as each side knew what was at stake. Charlene, a woman from the district whom I had never met, was at the table when we got there. She chatted with the other administrators amicably, but never once looked our way until the meeting started. Each person introduced themselves around the table. I smiled and indicated the food was for them. They offered tight smiles in return and allowed Charlene to lead the conversation. Her false, bright smile indicated she was here on a mission. As protocol dictated, each specialist gave her report and the teacher followed. Erik had to kick me under the table several times when I was about to interrupt. Our predetermined meeting protocol had been that we would let them speak first and then explain what we wanted and expected.

They laid out Owen's shortcomings and discussed what he couldn't do, articulating the milestones he hadn't reached. There is nothing more disheartening than sitting in a room with professionals who talk about your child's inability to learn and grow as if they were discussing a new product, tearing it apart piece by piece in their evaluation. At the conclusion of the lengthy report, I mustered up my courage.

"We want inclusion," I said, my voice smaller than I wanted it to be in the vacuum of silence. Charlene turned to us, full wattage on her smile. She dropped her voice an octave and gave me her best sympathetic expression.

"Why would you want that for your child?" She paused as if the silence would force me to feel shame and embarrassment for my bold ask. "Do you want him to fail? Would you like to see him falling so far behind his peers? What kind of parent wants that? We are the professionals; we understand your child's needs." I felt my stomach curdle as she continued to talk.

"Inclusion would only make Owen feel bad about himself, and he would likely lash out in frustration and anger. We see a lot of undesirable behaviors crop up when that happens." Having no other experience with which I could compare this to, I felt I was looking into a mirror of truth she was holding up, and I was forced to see everything I didn't want to admit about Owen. He would never catch up. He would fail, just like she said. They were the experts after all, right? My foundation was shaken, as was I.

I threw my voice into the ring again. "Fine, but we want our son in a class that is higher functioning. A place where he can make progress."

"Of course. We can manage that, right?" Charlene looked at her peers for confirmation. She had evaded full inclusion, and her victory was hidden in the smile she directed at me.

Our first and only stop was Riverside Elementary, which was

closer to our house than his current school, and the class seemed fairly motivating. The teacher allowed us time to watch what the kids were learning, and we accepted his placement, feeling confident that this was the next right step. That false sense of security was blown the first day I took Owen to school. The teacher stopped me at the door.

"Where's his aide?" she asked. I looked at her, confused.

"What do you mean? It's a Special Day Class. We don't get an aide for this class." She pointed to several adults who were mixed in with the kids sitting at the tiny desks.

"All my kids have aides, even those who don't need them. You march right to the principal's office and tell him you need an aide."

I didn't understand. We hadn't been told any of this when we observed her class in the spring. We told her our son had Down syndrome. Why was she questioning us now? I went to the principal's office and requested a meeting. Days went by and nobody contacted us. An uneasiness settled in as I began to get reports from the school: Owen was disruptive. He wasn't able to manage the class. I felt as if the teacher was deliberately making it a miserable experience for Owen. He seemed to like the class, and the kids in it.

One afternoon, Owen had been sent to the principal's office for stripping down to his underwear and encouraging others to do the same. It didn't sound like something Owen would do, and when I questioned him, he mumbled something about a wrestling contest. The next day, one of the aides in the class pulled me aside and told me what really happened. Another boy challenged him to a sumo wrestling contest, and when he told Owen they had to take their shirts off—like the real wrestlers—Owen pulled off his shirt off and squared up. The teacher came back and sent Owen to the principal's office, embellishing the scenario by telling the staff it was not just his shirt he took off but all his clothes.

"She doesn't like him in her class because if he doesn't have an aide, which means she has to work with him. That's why she prefers that all the kids have aides. Your kid is fine," the aide whispered.

Every other day we were told of some new, inappropriate thing

Owen had done, and I was unable to fight the onslaught of a teacher who wanted him out of her class.

In October, we met with the IEP team. The teacher and a few other administrators from the district sat across from us in a stifling room. I couldn't breathe. She had such disdain for Erik, for Owen, and for me. I could feel the heat of her dislike waft across the table toward me. I had come to the conclusion that if she felt such loathing for Owen, it would only hurt him.

"It's like working for a boss who doesn't like you," I told Erik as we pondered our next move. "They spend every moment wondering how they can trip you up at your job."

We moved him to the only available placement at a school in Van Nuys, where I felt like, if nothing else, he would learn to read. He was in second grade by now, and I felt time slipping away as his peers zoomed ahead. Even Tess, who was in preschool, was reading beginner books. I knew that second grade was a bust for him, and I had already begun the process of digging deeper into what exactly I needed to get him into full inclusion. A slow anger was simmering in me as I watched my beautiful boy continue to live every day with a smile, regardless of the situation, while I fumed inside.

The school he bounced to had one moderate-to-severe class placement left, and I could sense his inability to understand what was happening. I hadn't really taken into account his feelings about any of this. I'd only used him as a pawn to navigate what I thought would work for him. Each step made me reluctant to take the next as we slowly walked onto yet another school yard with unfamiliar faces, the language a blend of English and Spanish, and another teacher who was overwhelmed with too many kids amid the spectrum of disabilities. The look on Owen's face must have mirrored my own, but I refused to make eye contact and resolutely walked him into an educational setting that lacked any joy for him. The decision weighed heavily on me, and though I tried to make the best of it—by meeting the teacher and sending treats—I was unnerved when I walked with him onto campus and he fell behind, his gait becoming slower and slower. Perhaps that is when I felt the stirring of a dormant anger.

One morning, I said goodbye to Owen and stopped the teacher to speak with her for a moment. She said he was doing fine, but her attention was on three other students as she spoke to me. Realizing I'd get no information from her, I walked away. Moments later, though, I had an idea, so I turned the corner and circled back. I wanted to see what the first part of Owen's day looked like. The teacher, who appeared to be in her early twenties, forgot about me the minute I stepped away. She didn't even consider that I might spy on her class. As I watched, she turned to Owen, handed him his favorite Scooby Doo DVD (he was obsessed with it) and told him to go play on the apparatus. He loped along and swung himself up on the apparatus, hanging upside down, looking at his DVD. I was appalled. Was this her way of teaching? I flushed with anger, and the next day I repeated my actions. The same thing happened. Strike two.

I asked if I could observe Owen in class, since his morning was spent with one teacher and his afternoon was spent with a second teacher. I sat in the back of the class and watched as he checked out, not because he wasn't on their level, but there was no dynamic energy in the classroom. I felt a deep sorrow for my son. There he was, sitting with so many kids, yet clearly he was left alone in his thoughts while the teacher called out letters. They weren't even trying to teach the kids to learn to read yet, and I watched the bent head of my son, lost in a classroom designed for kids like him. This was so far from what I had imagined. So far from the promise I felt was extended by the school district in lieu of full inclusion. Where was the teacher-student interaction? The dynamics? Even the eye contact? My son was learning to accept what was never a perfect fit for him, and the window of enthusiasm in his eyes was slowly closing. But not anymore, not on my watch. I wasn't going to sit idly by and watch my son disappear.

I waited until spring, as there was no alternative for him, and our annual IEP meeting was scheduled. This time, I felt more empowered as I faced the district team. There was only one thing I wanted out of this meeting: full inclusion. We had moved to a neighborhood specifically for the highly rated school just a few blocks from us, and I was done sending my son miles away to school. He had no friends, nobody lived close by, and I felt as if my worst nightmare had come true: he was among the segregated few because of his disability.

The meeting took place at the school he was placed in. I recognized the woman, Charlene, who had twisted my vote for full inclusion into a placement in a Special Day Class. I made a point to smile broadly at her and reintroduce myself, shaking her hand much too firmly for comfort. She caught a whiff of my attention, and I once again urged the staff to eat the food I had brought.

We started off with the same agenda as always: each therapist and teacher read their very long, very detailed report as we all listened in silence. The district had their own tools to throw you off track: first, bore the hell out of you with goals; second, give minor lip service to incremental achievements and future goals; third, argue over therapist time counted out in minutes, not hours, until you thought you would go crazy with the sameness of it all.

Until placement recommendation came. The district and teachers agreed that Owen should stay in a Special Day Class, moderate to severe, which is where he was currently parked. My ears burned with the fury that had been slowly stoked over the last few months as my son learned nothing in their carefully contrived classroom setting. When Charlene looked at us for confirmation, I said the words she didn't want to hear—again.

"We want full inclusion." I could swear a look passed between her and her colleague. She smiled briefly.

"We've been through this before. He hasn't achieved the goals we thought he would, but I'm sure we could find another placement for him. A segue class."

I had segued him all over the city, and nothing had worked. I was done with their psychological warfare to keep my kid out of the neighborhood school that was just down the street. It was the school that parents extolled while I felt like a kid looking into a candy store, Owen's hand tucked in mine.

"Inclusion," I said again. I folded my hands over my chest and looked at the clock. The minutes ticked by slowly and loudly as the air grew thick with silence. Erik and I glanced at each other, a conspiratorial smile between us.

I had heard her spiel the year before, and the year before that. She had successfully gotten into my mind and made me wonder, *Am I a bad parent? Do I want to fail my child?* But this time, she hadn't counted on the fact that I was no longer a sure thing. I had seen what her "segue classes" had done for my child, and I was not happy.

I continued to wait, sensing everyone's discomfort. I said it again, just to be sure she heard it. I'll admit it was also because I wanted to see her squirm.

"Full inclusion." Our parenting union was having one of its most shining moments. Erik smiled.

"I think my wife and I agree that full inclusion is the best path for our son." We waited again. They weren't giving in, and we weren't backing down. I sat there, remembering how a therapist we had when Owen was three had shared a trick to get a verbal answer from Owen: ask him a question, then wait, even if our instinct was to keep talking. The time it took for our little standoff couldn't have been more than a few minutes, but it felt like an hour.

Finally, Charlene spoke. "I can't change your mind?"

I smiled. "Full inclusion."

She sighed, clearly irritated, then turned to her colleague. "Call in the inclusion specialist," she said. We sat there, Erik and I awkwardly making small talk. But our standoff was worth it because a few minutes later the inclusion specialist walked in.

"They're all yours," said Charlene, who then gathered her paperwork, nodded to us, and left. I felt a hesitant victory. I had bucked the system. Deep down, I knew something had inherently changed within me that would define not only Owen, but Erik and me too.

A few months later, after the paperwork had been signed, I called the local school and asked to speak to the principal. I told him that my son would be attending second grade in the fall and that he had Down syndrome.

"I don't think we have a class for special needs until third grade," he said.

"No, we are doing full inclusion," I explained.

"Well, he's not my student yet, so I can't speak to you on what that would look like."

"No problem," I responded. "I'm calling because you might want to write my name down. I have a feeling we are going to get to know each other really well."

I was preparing myself for a battle I might not have to fight, I realized, but I was going to make sure I was wearing my armor if it came to a head. A few weeks later, we showed up at the school to enroll him. An older woman at the desk said hello, and we slid our paperwork to her.

"I see it says he has an IEP?" she questioned.

I handed it to her. "Yep, he has Down syndrome."

Her smile went a little sour. "Well, this is going to be fun!" she said, her voice full of false cheer.

As we walked away, I felt almost giddy with delight because this was starting to feel like the right decision. He was finally going to be part of the community, not bussed away to some other campus miles from home. I needed to keep walking this path if for no other reason than I felt better, more grounded. He would now be close to our home in the neighborhood we had chosen.

Chapter Twenty-Three

Those first few months of school were not easy for me or Owen. The behaviors Owen had learned in his classes for the last three years now translated to complete disruption in his new class. His aide, Ms. Baker, was a petite, wiry woman, whose energy matched his. She mentioned to me how odd it was that he seemed to have traits more closely associated with autism, even though he didn't have that diagnosis. He sang along in class whenever he wanted. He rolled around, bumping up against other students when they had carpet time. He pushed over his pencil cup daily, disrupting the class. His teacher was unapologetic when she called a meeting with us and the principal. She sat across from us, arms crossed over her chest, her face obstinate.

"He doesn't belong here," she declared. "He doesn't belong in my classroom, and he doesn't belong in this setting."

I felt the searing anger start in my belly and rise up. I was deliberate with my words as I pasted a smile on my face.

"Then where does he belong? What setting is 'right' for him? We have tried every setting that LAUSD sent us to. This is where it stops. *You* are who it stops with. I'm not trying anywhere else that might be more appropriate. It's up to you, our home school, to figure this out. He deserves full inclusion just like any other kid. Tag, you're it!"

The venom in my words was pointed, and the assistant principal tried to soothe the exchange of words between us.

"Okay, let's not get out of hand. We'll figure this out. We can manage this together."

That meeting was a turning point for me—another victory. Without the hard-fought truth that Owen deserved to be in an inclusive setting, I would not have had the fuel to continue to try—for his sake, for my sake, for the sake of the next kid with Down syndrome, and the next. There was no "other" place for him. I wanted him to acclimate to our world, the real world.

My fear was that if he couldn't manage this scenario, then what was left? The difference was that we had found the place where typical kids were learning; there was so much energetic vibration that he had not been privy to. Once he began mixing with typical kids, his whole being changed. As I examined the situation over and over, mulling over the previous scenarios he was in, it finally occurred to me why his behaviors had escalated. For starters, Owen had not gotten worse. His behaviors had simply become cemented as habits because he had been spending a big chunk of his day with kids whose norm included those undesirable behaviors. He had never actually been in a typical classroom since he was in preschool. That moment of clarity led me to realize he had done exactly what he was good at: processed his world visually, internalized it, and then produced that visual. Because his world had been kids with special needs, that is what he acclimated to. Now we had a chance for him to become more like a typical child by mimicking how typical children acted. But first, we had to find a way for Owen to identify what "typical" looked like.

The assistant principal met with me after school the next day. She was slowly becoming my confidante, my fellow warrior, as she mulled over how to make it work for Owen. She never once backed down from our position that this was the last station for Owen. We had made too many stops along the way that didn't service his needs.

"I have a theory I would like to try," she offered. "But only if it's okay with you." She told me about a study utilizing reverse inclusion where a child was put in a class with kids a few years younger but on the same mental level, thereby allowing the child to understand what he was asked to do.

"When do we start?" I thought her idea was brilliant, and the recommended teacher was a sweet, warm, passionate kindergarten teacher. Upon approval from the principal, Owen's aide took him every day for two weeks to a kindergarten class for a few hours a day. As Owen looked around and saw what they were doing, he mixed in with the kids and followed them. These kids were Tess's age, and Owen spent the rest of his day at home with her, so it was an instant recognition for him.

After two weeks, he returned to his regular second grade class, and the report came back to me that it had worked. He followed what the others were doing. He stopped acting out in class, and he was listening. My heart soared with pride because my brilliant boy had done what I knew he could do all along: adapt to the world around him. Never was I happier than to see him walk out of a classroom with twenty other second graders, then run to greet me with a big hug.

Chapter Twenty-Four

When I became a parent, I didn't expect my friendships to change, so for the first few years of Owen's life, I kept the same circle of friends. But as he grew, and I adjusted for his disability and added more kids to my family, the dynamics of my life altered, and some friends naturally slipped away. I was busy and so were they. I didn't recognize the altered landscape I had slipped into until it was time to confront elementary school and Owen's place in it. New friendships for Owen became front and center and mirrored what I was feeling. Yes, I had the mom's group I had created, but outside of our once-a-month meetings, there were no spontaneous get-togethers, no meetups for coffee, and rarely did I get asked out to dinner. Who was going to organize new friends for me?

I deflected the loneliness and set my mind to the task at hand. I could populate his life with friends, and that would help fill the void. But how do you ask other parents to have a play date with your son with Down syndrome when they have no idea who he is? Most of these kids had been in school together since kindergarten, and parents had formed these indelible bonds over volunteer hours in their kinder classrooms. Most lived in the neighborhood and arranged play dates. It was as if we had moved to a new town and had to start over again. Even though we had been living in the neighborhood since he was three, the years of bussing him off to school had extracted us from any opportunities to meet local kids his age.

Most days, I waited outside his classroom on a painted bench, watching a few random kids return to their classroom, a luxurious half hour of time to myself before the bell rang and chaos ensued. New to the school, I didn't realize parents hung around and let their kids play on the field before heading home. I said hi to a few parents here and there, but I felt a bit like a ghost on campus. Was it that I wanted to fit in or I wanted Owen to fit in? I watched parents collect their children and walk in groups, laughing and making plans. I had no plans. I took Owen home after school, where Tess and Axel were waiting. Was I hoping for instant access to new friends? Perhaps. Did I think life was different on the other side of the "ability" fence? Absolutely.

I turned to the Internet and lurked on chat boards where parents talked about making a picture book of their child they distributed to the class. I didn't have the bandwidth to create a picture book, so I wrote a letter to the parents, essentially explaining who my child was: I spoke of his love of Scooby Doo and the band One Direction, and gave a simple explanation of what Down syndrome was so they could talk to their child. In a school of almost one thousand kids, Owen was the only kid with Down syndrome, so I knew there would be questions. I enclosed a copy of the "Welcome to Holland" essay written by Emily Perl Kingsley, given to me when Owen was a newborn. As a parent of a child with Down syndrome, her essay gave voice to what it felt like to be a parent of a child with a disability. After the letter was distributed, parents began reaching out, welcoming us (and Owen specifically) and a few offered a play date with their child. Friendship: check.

At the same time, I was juggling the dynamics at home with the three kids and struggling to interpret Owen's mental capability. My apologies to other parents because he often didn't "understand" playdate etiquette was wearing on me. I wanted to be able to just insert him into a group of kids, or drop him off at a playdate, without having to explain his differences or his lack of understanding. But perhaps I had underestimated him . . . and Tess was the bridge to that understanding.

If there was one part of my day I would gladly skip, it was the kids' bedtime. I chided myself for not wanting to put them to bed, read to them, and shepherd them into good nighttime habits. I loved many parts of raising kids, but I dreaded these hours. The endurance skills it took to cajole three kids up the stairs and into pajamas, then the toothbrushes and glasses of water, and "I'm hungry" would prolong it. Then one of them would slink behind my back and head downstairs again. It was like trying to keep puppies in a basket when all they wanted to do was leap out and run back down the hall. They slid out of my reach like eels, and I sighed wearily, sitting on a bed, waiting for them to come back so we could read a story. But each one had to have their own story, and after that they wanted alone time with both of us to say goodnight. Inside, I hated myself for not wanting to spend time with them, for not having patience, and I tried to remind myself how lucky I was to have children to put to bed. But more than anything, I just wanted a glass of wine and a chance to unwind by myself at the end of a long day.

Out of desperation one night, I told Owen and Tess we were going to play a pajama game. I had already poured myself a healthy glass of wine.

Both of them sat at the bottom of the stairs in anticipation. "Let's see who can put on their pajamas the fastest. Run upstairs, put them on, and come back down to this step. Got it?"

The two nodded solemnly. I thought the game would result in both of them finishing at about the same time, or possibly Tess winning because even though she was two years younger, her motor skills were more advanced than his. I counted them down and they took off up the stairs. Checking on them, they both refused help, so I went back downstairs, delighted with my new approach. I waited. Owen, despite having to take the stairs slower than Tess, beat her and sat down. Tess came down the stairs and sat next to him. Owen had a big smile on his face, and I congratulated him.

"Good job, buddy! You did it!" I was so proud of him, and he was beaming with his own sense of pride. Then I glanced at Tess.

"Owen won," she said and started to cry. "I wanted to win. I wanted to win!" She bawled as the smile on Owen's face disappeared. Without a word, Owen stood and went upstairs. I could tell he was bewildered and sad. I tried to calm Tess down and keep my anger toward her at bay, but eventually I left her to sob it out as I went upstairs. Owen was in his room, redoing his pj's.

"Tess can do it. She can win. See? I'm slower," I heard him saying. My heart broke for him as he crept into bed and pulled the covers over his head. I tried to give him a hug, but he pushed me aside. Maybe it was the fact that we hadn't shied away from telling him he had Down syndrome. Or maybe he was noticing the difference between himself and the other kids in his class. Maybe it was none of this. I just wanted to find a logical reason to reassure myself that I was doing the best I could as a parent.

"Go away," he said, pointing at the door.

I went into Tess's room, suffused with anger but unsure what to do. Scolding her for being upset about losing didn't feel like the right parenting move to me. She brushed her teeth and, sensing my anger, got into bed. I asked if she wanted to hear a story, and she nodded. I told her about a little girl named Tess who hurt her brother, even though he adored her.

"But, Mommy, I wanted to win," she said in her tiny voice. I tried to explain that she can't always win, but in her mind, that rationale didn't make sense. A moment later, Owen appeared at Tess's door. He came into her room and gave me a wordless hug. My heart lurched. He ignored Tess and went back to bed.

I patiently explained to Tess again that Owen wasn't as smart as she was, and that his brain didn't work the same way as hers, but sometimes he could win at a game too.

"I know . . . because he has Down syndrome," she said, enunciating the words. "But I still wanted to win." She wouldn't acquiesce. As I left the room, I heard her frighteningly small voice follow me out.

"Goodnight, Mommy."

I was puzzled at this standoff: two kids who love each other so much but don't know how to cross that bridge to forgiveness. Because of the emotional drama of the night, Tess crept into my bed to sleep with us. When I woke up, she looked at me with one eye open, not sure what my mood was. I smiled and kissed her, and she smiled back. It was different with Owen that morning. I went into his room and gently patted his back.

"Come on, buddy, it's time to get up."

"I don't want to go to school," he said. This was a kid who asked every night if he was going to school tomorrow. Not so today. That is when I knew he totally understood what happened last night. The memory of it all hadn't faded. It had likely seeped into his dreams and woven itself around the lingering edges of sleep. I tried again.

"Come on, Owen, it's a school day." He reluctantly pulled the covers back. I got him up and helped him dress. Tess came down the hallway slowly.

"Kiss and make up, you two," I said, holding my breath.

Owen would not look at Tess; his eyes remained downcast. Tess went to Owen and knelt in front of him.

"Good morning, Owen. Can I have a hug?" Owen raised his eyes and the hint of a smile was there. Then he opened his arms and they both fell to the floor, hugging. Slowly, I breathed out. The crisis was over. What struck me was that Owen was willing to give the win back to Tess, but she had hurt him deeply, and he needed time to process his feelings. This proved to me that his mental acuity was greater than I had hoped, allowing him to process hurt just like anyone else. The realization was dawning on me that Owen understood what was happening. Despite being upset, he was processing resolution and forgiveness.

I now knww that my role in this scenario was pivotal. I was proud of myself for letting it play out, something I had been reluctant to do up until now. By holding back and letting them figure it out, I got a glimpse into Owen's understanding of relationships, which made it clear to me that his frequency was set to normal just like other kids. Owen knew his diagnosis made him slow, but that didn't deter him from managing the intricacies of a relationship. The ability to embrace a wide range of emotions—happiness, sadness, anger, fear—gave me another key to unlocking the myriad facets of Owen's ability to understand.

Ever since Owen started full inclusion, Erik and I had a motto: *life is not a special needs class.* The early years were harder to allow him freedom because we hovered over him day after day. There were eyes and ears around us constantly: in the neighborhood, at school, in the park. Therapists, teachers, and our friends were there to lend a hand when he wandered away. But as he grew, the natural affinity of a parent is to allow more freedom, to give a wider berth to explore, to help understand boundaries.

Against my natural instinct to protect, protect, protect, I understood that as Owen grew, he would need a wider landscape to test his limitations. I started with less supervision at the playground, or allowing him to go into a public bathroom by himself. (A silent thanks to all the random dads I asked to check on him in the stall.) I had to resist the urge to follow him around and make sure he was okay and knew how to find his way back to me.

Fundamentally, Owen's cognitive level with academics was parked back in first grade, but at he grew and progressed, his empathic skills were through the roof. He was a kid who could discern a friend in need of a hug, or find the person who was sitting alone and plop down next to them. He told jokes that made sense on a deeper level than some kids got, but adults understood. His quirky behavior created a following of kids who wanted to be near him, who wanted to bask for a bit in his aura, a Zen-like quality that was hard to describe but seemed to come from a deeper bliss that anchored him. Unlike other kids, Owen didn't worry about school or friends, and stress wasn't a word he understood. He walked through his life doing what was asked of him, but his inner vibration caused people to want to be around him, to circle him, to include him. Was I aware of it? In my own life, his good nature was always around me, providing a sense of calm and peace when I was with him, and his smile always soothed whatever agitated me. It didn't occur to me that others felt it, too, until parents approached me, or neighbors reached out, or teachers tried to define it. He provided an energy that few people could describe, but it was there, bubbling below the surface. My Buddha.

Chapter Twenty-Five

As days swirled together, syncing up school and work became easier, especially when Axel joined Tess and Owen in elementary school. I found a rhythm in my days I had not known before, and time inevitably flew by. They were growing so fast, stepping into their personality one grade at a time, until I found myself at the first last day of Owen's elementary school. During this last year, I was desperate to hold on to the womb-like comfort of the school. I wasn't the only parent. We all faced the leap to middle school, when the world begins to lap at our doorstep as they begin the bold steps into the next phase of their lives.

That final year, Erik and I walked our kids into school together, greeting other parents as we dropped each child off at their respective classrooms. Owen's fifth grade teacher, Ms. Shahine, was new to the school. She was petite, with thick and wavy brown hair, and every day she stood at the doorway dressed in brightly colored dresses, tailored for her tiny figure like a diminutive doll, greeting all her students. Her class contained all the kids Owen had grown up with the past three years, including a girl named Lauren. Since that first day of inclusion, when they sat next to each other in class, the two had formed an irreplaceable bond. They could be seen together around school, and he would smile and call her "his girlfriend." The gift of this particular classroom was a bonding experience for not just Owen, but Ms. Shahine and her students as well. It was not only her first year, which came with its own learning curve; it was the kids' year of firsts and lasts, including an overnight trip and a graduation ceremony.

In the spring, as matriculation hovered over our heads, the fifth graders went on a three-day camping trip with their class. Owen had never attended sleep-away camp or been away from us. Ever. Naturally, I met with the teacher.

"He'll be fine," she said. "I think it's a perfect time for him to try camp." Indecision must have shown in my eyes because she looked at me and said, "I will not let anything happen to him. Trust me."

Despite her assurance, Erik and I visited the camp and the staff. The manager said they often have kids on the spectrum as well as other disabilities who come for summer camp, so they were used to accommodations. He pointed out a cabin one of us could stay in during the trip if we felt we needed to be there, as a last resort. The camp was well thought out and fairly self-contained. I wanted so badly for this to work out—for Owen, for us, and for all the kids he knew so well who wanted him on that trip.

The morning they were to leave, I dropped him off at the crack of dawn, greeting other parents and teachers as we huddled into our jackets, steaming coffee in hand.

Ms. Shahine came to me and looked me in the eyes. "We've got plenty of teachers to help out. I know it's scary to let your first child go away by himself. But please, don't worry." I hugged her tightly.

"Thank you," I whispered, not daring to believe that Owen was going to be away from us for three whole days.

It was odd not to have Owen in our house those next few days, singing at the top of his lungs, waking us up with hugs and smiles. But I felt as if a tiny bit of growth had just happened within me too. We had separated ourselves so that we could help him grow up and out. This trip served as a starting point for us to sever our codependence on him too. I went out on a limb to allow him to experience camp like any other fifth grader, and my fears abated as soon as he left because there was nothing more I could do. The return of my child was a milestone I had never fathomed would happen when he was a baby.

The windows of the bus were crowded with kids waving and smiling as parents milled around, greeting their campers. I felt tears prick my eyes as Owen came off the bus with Lauren, and the two of them gave each other a big hug. He had returned, and he could now rightly step into the role of oldest brother, having completed a rite of passage the other two had not. He seemed different somehow, more mature, and I smiled to myself thinking, *He's just like any other kid.*

I fought battles so he could be treated like every other kid, not knowing if the chances we took would allow him to flourish or fail. In actuality, aside from one extra chromosome, he was as regular and as unique as any other child. Nobody could walk in his shoes on that last leg of his elementary school journey. He walked proudly, boldly, and happily to the finish line. In my earliest days when he was a baby, I could not have imagined this euphoria, this example of winning. He won the race to be born. I won the fight to have him included. On graduation day, he won his freedom from all the invisible chains of society holding him back. He had broken the stigma for himself and for future kids with Down syndrome who would come to this school or another school.

Chapter Twenty-Six

Erik and I had always been firm believers in organized sports as we were raised in families where sports were prevalent. I grew up with my dad coaching my brothers in football, basketball, and baseball, and my sisters and I played softball. Erik played basketball through junior college. Standing at six feet seven, he was on the watch list for Washington State by the tenth grade.

The summer of the 2012 Olympics was the year that Michael Phelps took home the most gold medals for swimming. As we often did during the Olympics, we recorded different sports to watch later. I was spending more time at work, and Erik was busy managing the kids, so we set Owen in front of the TV to watch the replay of the Olympics. He learned how to use the remote control and kept returning again and again to Michael Phelps's races. He replayed them in slow motion, and then forward in slow motion. This went on for weeks, and I felt a twinge of mom guilt. But it kept him entertained, so I let it slide because I saw how uncomplicated he was at that moment. He was fascinated, like the rest of the world, by someone who was taking the Olympic world by storm.

Sometimes I felt like I was peering at Owen through a microscope, waiting for him to unfold, to flower. I panicked that he wouldn't accomplish the next milestone. Then, just like that, he achieved it. My way of laying out plans for him only frustrated me, not him. Subconsciously, I was still rejecting the gift that he was, the package of uniqueness that was his to present to me. Even though I thought Owen needed my help, he was managing to show his unique personality and traits all on his own. I was his creator, but he was painting his world with colors of his own choosing.

A few weeks later, the neighbors invited us over to swim. Owen sat on the ledge with about two feet of water in it, as he usually did. The other two were gamely learning to swim, beginning with the doggy paddle, exactly the way I learned when I was five. I looked at Owen as he put his face under water again and again, holding his breath for as long as he could, which could be up to a minute sometimes.

"Does Owen know how to swim?" my neighbor asked.

I glanced at him and shook my head no. "You're nine, Owen, when are you going to learn to swim?" I had given up, as lessons at the YMCA didn't help him, and it wasn't on my list of priorities anymore. Some kids just take to water; other kids have a different kind of fear before they find their safe space. Was I looking at Owen's swimming this way? I have to confess I was wondering if being a child with Down syndrome held him back in everything.

"Mom, I can swim," he said, his head down as he swirled his hand in the water. "I can swim like Michael Phelps."

"Then show me," I countered, not believing for a minute he was going to swim.

He jumped off the ledge so he was standing in the water. Then, just like Michael Phelps would do, he dove underwater, wriggled his body, and came up for air as his arms initiated the butterfly stroke until he reached the side of the pool. He touched the side wall and stood up.

"See? I can swim. Just like Michael Phelps."

I sat in the hot sun, sweat dripping down my back, astonished. I had never seen him swim, especially not in that advanced capability. Then my mind replayed all the hours he had spent watching Michael Phelps on TV. The endless replay of him swimming the length of Olympic size pools in slow-motion increments. Owen had found another superpower. He had internally visualized swimming that stroke, auto-second by auto-second, on the TV. His mind had visually taught him, and today, he had proved that yes, "he can swim just like Michael Phelps."

Erik and I looked at each other, and just like that, swimming was on our radar. Within the next two weeks, I found Owen a Special Olympics swim team in Pasadena, the Pasadena Ducks. I was more nervous than Owen, but the minute we got to the Olympic-size outdoor pool and introductions were made, Owen stripped down to his swim trunks and got in the water. It was as if he knew this was where he belonged. Coach Jen introduced herself to me, as did other young women and men who volunteered their time to get in the water with swimmers whose disabilities ranged from autism to cerebral palsy to other issues I couldn't diagnose by sight.

In the beginning, Owen was afraid of the length of the pool and could only manage the first half of the lane. As the pool got deeper, the water became colder, and it was as if he knew that the depth was now farther away. His coach coaxed him gently, holding his arms as she got him to swim the length of the pool. I watched the lessons, the gentleness, the praise, and Owen swam hard for an hour. She was the beginning of my ability to recognize the warriors who populate the world we live in. Her gentleness with my son didn't belittle him; it empowered him. She treated him with respect. I watched, and my sight took on a clarity I hadn't known, sweeping away the illusion that only I could mold and create him. My son was tapping into his own potential under another's guidance, and I was giddy with the potential I saw in him.

After the first session, Jen came over to me. "How long has Owen been swimming?" I told her how he started and that we hadn't really put him in any formal training.

"I'm impressed! His base stroke is really good. He can use some tweaking, but as soon as he learns to swim the length of the pool, he'll advance significantly."

Her words warmed me, and the drive now didn't seem so long

and daunting. I learned to take advantage of the track behind the pool so I could run while Owen swam. Some nights I sat for a while with the parents, but we barely spoke to each other; if we did, it was a quick hello. We were a mixed assortment: an older couple who watched their daughter and soon learned to follow me to the track so they could walk; a younger woman who barely looked up as she worked incessantly; and a father who lingered on the perimeter of the pool deck, his son the most vocal and curious of the kids.

Owen took such pride in his sport, never failing to show up and get right in the pool, despite the chill of the water during cold spring nights. I relished the time I got to spend with my son. We bonded on the long drive during evening traffic, and I could count on some "me" time on the college track behind the pool as I watched the sun set over the San Gabriel Mountains. For that hour, I could forget about work, home, and the giant to-do list in my mind that nagged at me incessantly.

The dedication Owen took on with swimming became a source of pride for all of us. He told his friends at school and his teachers, and as the weeks went by, his strength and power became clear when he was in the water. He understood the freedom water gave him, and it propelled him to push himself more and more. He wasn't judged by his mentality in the pool, only his athleticism.

One night his coach decided to teach him the backstroke. She pulled me aside after practice. "I am astounded at how well he picked up the backstroke. It's as if he knew the stroke already."

I told her the backstory on swimming and the influence of Michael Phelps.

"You have a rock star swimmer on your hands," she said.

Owen's first swim meet was scheduled for the end of February, but cold and flu season was in full swing. I prayed every night that he stayed healthy. It wasn't unusual for Owen to be the first in our family to catch a cold, and for it to linger the longest. But with so much going on in his body, just one health incident would capsize the boat. Mid-month he developed a cold and it progressed to an ear infection as it typically did. We plied him with antibiotics, which usually did the trick, but this illness refused to leave his body.

Erik took him to the doctor again, but this time sent an emergency text while I was in a meeting, which is the worst place to receive a text that says, "Call me ASAP." There is the awkward attempt to sidle out of the meeting, trying not to interrupt the speaker as eyeballs track my every move.

"The doctor doesn't like Owen's oxygen levels," Erik explained on the phone.

"What does that mean?" I said, tapping my pen on my desk, impatience surging as I realized they had been at the doctor's office for two hours.

"They may have to admit him to the hospital. They won't let him go home until his oxygen levels rise." My mind started mapping out the time. The other two kids were about to finish school and needed to be picked up. I raced out of work and met Erik at the doctor's office. Owen was sitting in a chair sporting an oxygen mask. His listless demeanor told the whole story. The doctor came in and checked his vitals again.

"I can't seem to get Owen's oxygen levels up, so I'm going to admit him into the hospital," he said. "It looks like pneumonia."

Fear prickled my neck. My mind skipped wildly as worst-case scenarios pinged back and forth. The doctor agreed to let Erik take Owen to the hospital, and I left to pick up our other two kids from school. My actions were frenzied as I packed what I needed to stay at the hospital. I called Eva to see if she could watch the younger ones.

"I told you this would happen. The way you and Erik let the kids run around and wipe their noses on their sleeves," she said, the disdain in her voice obvious. Her righteousness was unnecessary and irritating.

"Never mind, I can send them to the neighbor's house," I began, but she quickly interrupted me.

"I suppose that's what I'm here for," she responded, promising to be at our house within the hour.

When I got to the hospital, Erik instructed me to hold the oxygen tubes under his nose, since Owen didn't like having the mask strapped on his face. I looked at him quizzically. "I'm supposed to hold these under his nose the whole time?" It didn't make sense, but Erik explained that Owen felt more comfortable this way. I shrugged, assuming the nurse had approved. But now I was uncomfortable holding my arm in front of his face. I slacked off when he was sleeping. Nurses came in and out, checking his vitals. That night, we both slept fitfully. In the morning, I awoke early and walked over to his bed, immediately noticing a tinge of blue around his mouth. I quickly called the nurse.

"Is this normal?" I asked. "He's turning blue!" The nurse checked his oxygen levels and they were low—lower than they had been when he was first admitted.

"Your husband told me he wouldn't wear the oxygen mask, so I told him it was okay as long as he held the tubes under his nose. But it's not enough." Anger surged through me.

"Well, I'm the mom, and he's damn well going to wear the mask whether he likes it or not. He doesn't get to make that decision."

I grabbed the mask and leaned toward Owen, forcibly putting the mask on him. "You are going to wear this or you will die," I said, my voice taut. "We are going to do this my way now. Got it?"

The nurse looked at me. "I guess I should have talked to you instead of his dad."

I turned to her. "He's too soft with him. I'm not."

I was shaken. What if Owen hadn't survived the night? What if his oxygen levels had dropped so much that he had no breath anymore? The logical part of me knew that alarms would have gone off if he stopped breathing, but I was furious with my husband for catering to Owen. I know the kids loved how gentle he was with them, often allowing them to make decisions that I would not, but this was a time to put my foot down and be the parent. I was always the parent who yelled, took things away, set up consequences the kids didn't like. His way was to talk them through it. I was not going to talk. Shoving the plastic tubes up his nose was the only action necessary.

I set myself up on the extra bed and worked virtually from his hospital room for the next five days. When he was finally well enough to leave, we arrived home to welcome signs and balloons floating on the ceiling and a gooey cheese pizza from Quickies, his favorite restaurant. When the owners found out he was sick, they sent over a pizza to coincide with our return home.

A few weeks later his health was almost back to normal, and he competed in his first Special Olympics swim meet. A crowd of his friends from school gathered in the stands, cheering "Owen! Owen!" as he took his mark. He saw them and waved, ecstatic at his fans. A woman next to us leaned over and touched me on the arm. "My daughter's been swimming for years, and she's never had her friends come and watch. He's a lucky kid." I agreed and mouthed a silent prayer of gratitude that Owen could be here today, competing and receiving support from his friends on this brilliantly sunny day.

Chapter Twenty-Seven

The looming matriculation from elementary school to middle school for Owen collided with an imbalance in my place in the world. I changed companies with the elusive goal of more freedom, only to find my hands were tied more than ever, and the constant demands never let up. Some days it felt manageable, but that state was fluid and was quickly drowned out by underlying thoughts of imposter syndrome. I woke up early, tired even as my feet hit the floor, the clock timing me as I raced to make the kids' lunches, get them up and out of bed, then head out the door. Each day brought a sigh of relief as we pulled up a minute or two before the bell rang. Then I'd head back home and jump into another race as I readied myself for work, sometimes running on my treadmill for a quick ten-minute workout before I showered. Mentally, I scrolled through my day, hoping to find another ten minutes somewhere to take a walk. On days I couldn't leave the office, I traipsed up and down the stairs from the first floor to the third floor as often as I could, the mini workouts a hope that I could counteract the lethargy that ensued from constantly sitting at my desk. Lunch was almost always eaten at my desk, and by late afternoon I scrambled to finish the day's tasks so I could arrive home by the dinner hour.

Those last few years I spent in a corporate position can only be summed up as the angry years. Every evening when I arrived home, anger blinded me: Backpacks lay jumbled on the floor. Shoes were strewn everywhere. Dishes were unwashed in the sink. The kids always seemed to be lounging in front of the TV instead of doing homework. I felt defeated. But it wasn't really the home life that angered me; that was what took the brunt. My anger simmered all day long as I battled the constant inequalities at work. Nothing was ever good enough. Projects were never complete enough. And if they were, someone inevitably took credit for my work. Even as I worked harder and stayed longer to compensate, my motives were questioned, my absences noted. Any self-respect I had was slowly being whittled away.

Most nights, Erik had dinner on the table by the time I got home, but some nights I chose to head to the back room for a workout rather than eat with them, the need to physically move my body and push through the curdled anger seemed more important to me. My choices made him angry, and silence or a fight would ensue. I felt burdened by the weight of work and by an environment that was unhealthy for me mentally. I knew that he got the shaft, but I was completely expended beyond my limit, and partnership was an easy bucket to forgo. To add ease to my nights, I drank wine, pouring more than was necessary. I found solace in my nightly glasses of "liquid gold," as I called it, even as I knew it would make the next day's alarm more unwelcome than it already was. But with my special needs child, there was no blame game when I got home, only a bear hug and a kiss. I could revel in the easiness of that relationship instead of getting wrapped up in the who-did-what-today arguments that hovered over my life.

I was nervous about releasing my child into the next phase of school, even as I took the steps to craft what that would look like. During the middle school tour, our guide showed us an eighth grade classroom where I looked at boys with facial hair and bodies that had become too tight to sit in desk chairs. I was fascinated by their emerging manliness. I thought of Owen: my underdeveloped boy with Down syndrome who sported round glasses and loped along, sometimes skipping, as he sang out loud. How would he fit in with what appeared to be larger-than-life boys to men? I chastened myself for once again thinking too far ahead. It was an illusion. Once your child starts middle school, the days fly by and kids sprout up—like plants bursting out of the ground almost overnight. This was a world I had only vague recollections of, as though the years in between had cloaked my memories in a gauzy, yellowed curtain, drowning out the daily memories of middle school. Randomly, I caught a sharp scent of memories, a waft of perfume or a hint of sweat, the sloppy uniform clothes reminding me of my days in Catholic school. But I didn't have time for a surge of memories to invade my life now. My laser-focused task was to make sure Owen succeeded in this next phase of his life.

Of course, I had to set up a second tour to visit the Special Day Class, which I had been recommended to do (proving the point once again that a parent with special needs seems to always be doubling up on the workload). I was led through campus, around the back, and down a half-obscured sidewalk to a solitary building where two classrooms sat.

"Why is it so far away from everything else?" I asked.

The teacher was irritated by my questions. I had grown accustomed to this pattern. I asked uncomfortable questions and contradicted the norm, and no one was particularly happy to embrace my worldview for my son.

In my life before kids, I wouldn't have given it a second thought, and if my son had been typical, it wouldn't have occurred to me there was anything wrong with this picture. But to the warrior mom I had become, it was glaringly apparent that kids in the Special Day Class were segregated within the school. I wanted my son to be seen, to be a part of the world, not be hidden away. When I asked around, typical kids told me they had never seen anyone with Down syndrome on campus, yet here in these hidden classrooms, I counted at least four. Why was I so adamant I had to blaze a trail for Owen? He needed to fill the gaps in the world, in society, to show them that Down syndrome wasn't the worst thing to have. And the only place to start was here, in his own neighborhood school.

A nagging feeling that I was pushing him to be my ideal crept in. Was this my end game? Or his? Was fighting for inclusion for me, so I could toot my own horn and be the hero of the story? Parents told me that Owen was doing so well because we boosted his ability. I deflected that praise, knowing deep down Owen had the capacity to be more than what the textbooks said he could be. He just needed guidance, and I was the person who was chosen to lead the way. I was competitive, and since his birth, I kept stoking the fire, measuring him against others with his diagnosis, constantly recalibrating the tools he needed to succeed. Perhaps I wanted some of the glory and that's what kept me steering him, always adjusting for hiccups in the system.

To alleviate my scattered mind, I raced through my days, trying to complete and compete at the same time. I defaulted to constant busyness as a deflection for the emptiness I felt in the transition. Deep down, I didn't feel rooted despite all those years in elementary school that I thought would have yielded a constant group of friends, a revolving mix of play dates and grown-up dates. Instead, I felt untethered, drifting between different groups of friends, categorized, compartmentalized. I was a working mom, which put me in the group who barely showed up at school except for holiday concerts and weekend events. But I volunteered for almost everything, reprioritizing my schedule between work and home. I attended it all, and perhaps the confusion lay in my visibility; nobody else knew quite how to label me. My over-zealous approach left me on the sidelines, which made me wonder what I did or didn't do. Had I chatted enough, or too much? Was I too overbearing? Did they or didn't they want to hear about my job?

At an elementary school PTA meeting held at night so working moms could join, I stood in the back, sipping on a glass of wine. I didn't need to listen to the conversation. I had already been to the morning meeting, despite being late to work. In the morning, the PTA liaison scanned the group of us and spied me, confirming I would attend both meetings, which gave me a momentary sense of pride. I was needed. After all, I was a working mom, so naturally my presence at the later meeting would bridge the gap between the groups.

I glanced around, noting the moms listening in rapt attention. These were the parents who dropped off their kids in the carpool lane, sent checks instead of volunteering, and were meeting each other for the first time. I still felt uncomfortable, simultaneously fitting in with neither and both crowds. I whispered to the mom next to me, who I had met on a few occasions.

"Did you like the dip I brought?" My biggest decision of the day was spent on making a dip from scratch that I thought was worthy of this crowd.

"Mm-hmm," she said, her mouth partially full.

"Good, I wasn't sure if anyone would try it."

She laughed. "You're kidding, right? Everyone knows you're the rock star mom: three kids, a job, and Owen. Everything you do is 110 percent, so of course I'm going to try your dip!"

I was taken aback. Rock star mom? I let that roll around in my brain. Never had I thought of myself as having rock star status. But she had named it, and now I wondered if maybe rock star was my nemesis.

Then the day finally came . . . the morning of Owen's fifth grade culmination. My emotions wreaked havoc on my mind as I walked through the school door. This last day of elementary school would be bittersweet; parents who had been through this before cautioned me to slow down, clear my schedule, and remember this day because it only comes once. My battles for Owen at this juncture were over. We had planted the flag of victory as he approached this day. To really immerse myself in this special day for him, I specifically told my boss I was not available. For one single day, I wanted to think only of my family, not the endless requests from work. I wasn't sure what kinds of emotions the day would bring, and I wanted to give myself the space to allow for them, which was a big step for me.

Walking across the school's campus, my phone rang insistently. I looked to see it was my boss, and I politely ignored it. The realization that he felt it was okay for him to interrupt me on a day I asked him not to rankled me. As we were sitting down, waiting for the ceremony to start, my phone buzzed again. A slow anger enveloped me. It showed a lack of respect—for me, for my request, for my family. What was so God-almighty important? I was determined to have a day, one day, this day, and any infringement on that was now a direct attack on my own boundaries that for too long I had allowed others to encroach upon. I got up and walked away, answering the call, my voice shaking.

"Oh, hey, Suzanne, I was just calling to tell you that I have an issue with the wine you picked out for the event on Saturday night. I think we need to rethink what we are serving."

Wine? He called about my choice of wine for an event we were hosting three days from now? This was LA. Everything could be managed in three days. I was livid as I heard the ceremonial song begin in the background. I felt all the moments of disrespect rise up in my throat. *Steady*, I thought. *This is your job.*

"I can't talk right now. I am at my son's graduation. I told you that." I hung up as my hands were shaking and took a deep breath. The phone rang again.

His voice, in all its pleasantness, rattled me even further.

"I think our connection must be bad," he said, assuming that I would never hang up on him. "Like I was saying, we need to address the wine. I don't like what you picked out."

I stared at my phone, at the voice that wouldn't stop talking, on this day of all days, when I needed him to just shut up.

I took a deep breath. "I'll call you later. We can sort through this then. Honestly, I have to go." I hung up again and turned my phone on silent.

I wish I could say this wasn't my fault, but I had spent my whole adult life supporting my bosses, deferring to them. It was what I knew I was good at: the peacemaker role, placating egos, smoothing out the sharp edges. Here was another moment, etched in my mind, of the way I would walk him through, holding his hand, soothing him, using the right words to make him think it was his decision. Today, though, I had no time for the intricacies of the negotiation. It was my time, my day to see my son graduate.

I took my seat as the summer heat swelled and kids smiled shyly at their parents. Names were called and, one by one, with their sweet solemnity masking their nervousness, they walked up to receive their certificate. When Owen's name was called, his smile overtook his face as he walked up, hugged his teacher, then raised his fists in the air, his excitement a testimony to all those children and educators who had championed him for years. I heard a low hum begin and grow louder, and it took me a moment to realize the entire fifth grade class had stood up clapping and started chanting, "Owen! Owen! Owen!" Tears slid down my cheeks as I watched the class commemorate him in the best way they knew how: a tribute to who he was, Down syndrome and all.

After the ceremony, kids poignantly said goodbye, and the familiarity of the school and campus tugged at my heart as I realized this was my step into the next phase for Owen. Random bits of paper littered the yard while younger kids called to each other, playing tag or tetherball, unaware that they would be forced to exit their childhood one day too. We walked away, and I felt invisible hands pushing us out. The other two were still in their classrooms, biding their time until the last bell while we walked home with Owen. I felt lost, as if the familiar face of childhood had disappeared. My safe haven for him was gone, and we were left with a summer of unknowns.

Nobody could see the fragility that resided in me. My exterior was like leather, toughened by the years, but inside I felt like bone china, the slightest mishandling of my ego and I would crack. So much of my life with Owen had been a series of unknowns, and I surmounted each challenge, one by one. Yet I still struggled to trust all would be well; that my story would have a happy ending. There is no playbook, no manifest that comes with having a child, any child. Even today, I wonder where the book was for my life, for my rules, for my destiny. I suppose, ultimately, everyone must write their own.

Chapter Twenty-Eight

Something about the summers that follow graduation have always made me pause. There is a gap of unspecified direction, when the next place isn't quite real, but the memories of the last place you inhabited still remain, hovering. Bidding the safety of the former world goodbye, I shied away from any anticipation of what the new school year looked like. I still had two kids in elementary school, but it felt different. I felt different. Owen had lost the steady cocoon of friendship as they all dispersed to summer camps and different schools, while I felt my network of moms who embraced me and Owen drift away too.

Here was the next opportunity for me, though, the next point of entry: middle school. No matter how much I wanted to stay steeped in childhood, my kids would grow up, and it was time for the next step. A phase when puberty blooms and personalities emerge. I also had a second shot of making some new friends; oh, the irony, to be approaching fifty and still desperate to make friends.

On the first day of middle school, we stood in line with other kids, waiting for the teacher to open her door and greet us. I smiled tentatively at the other parents, who looked equally nervous. Owen recognized several kids he had been with in elementary school, and they all stood together, a summer of awkwardness between them. The teacher came out and stood at the top of the steps to her classroom with pink hair that filtered the gray in between, donning a Harry Potter cloak.

"Welcome, young wizards," she said, inviting them into the classroom.

Each day, Owen stepped a little more confidently into middle school, and so did I. Watching him disappear onto campus in those early days, I paused to contemplate what thoughts went through his head. When I asked if he was making friends, he grunted and turned back to his phone.

"I don't want to talk about it, Mom," he'd say, a response I would grow to know well when my two younger kids hit middle school. Typical teen.

His first IEP of middle school was called early, and the oh-so-repetitive question that had defined his placement year after year was voiced.

"Can you tell me why he's in my class?" the teacher asked. The battle had begun. In the past few months, I had come to terms with his lack of academic prowess, his inability—and sometimes unwillingness—to read. And despite hours of doing simple math, it was still puzzling to him. But I also had begun to shed the expectations, the belief that knowing how to dissect a sentence or multiply would never be crucial skills in Owen's life. Combined with the novelty of middle school that included an expansive campus, a rush of twice as many kids, and a revolving door of new teachers, middle school was a blizzard of sensory overload for any kid.

The attack on my son felt personal, as it always did. As he aged, I knew that sooner or later he would begin to discern this bias toward him.

"He's so far behind the other kids. Let's face it, he barely reads," the teacher who had volunteered to participate in his IEP said. "You do know about the Special Day Class on campus, right?"

In the latent summer heat, her blonde, wavy hair spilled onto her shoulders, reminding me of another teacher who brought up the same question years ago. It was as if I had been propelled back to that second-grade meeting, only this time, I had three years of inclusion under my belt. I knew in my heart it was no longer about the academics; it was about socialization. For Owen, life skills were the academics we were after, and you could only find those in full inclusion. I smiled, the mini-wars I had won in the past a gentle reminder inside me.

Calmly but politely, I replied to her. "You may not see him doing the same work, but everything you talk about in class, Owen is absorbing. I wouldn't underestimate him." Society as a whole has a way of underestimating kids with disabilities, and inclusion was my way to prove the institution wrong.

Shelly, his aide, caught up with me a few days later. "The teacher is trying really hard to engage him, but he keeps pushing her away."

I smiled as if bursting with a big secret. "He knows! He knows she doesn't want him in her classroom, and he's not going to give in." We laughed conspiratorially. I had stopped giving in long ago to teachers and administrators and professionals who thought they knew better than me. They were textbook people, swayed by papers and doctorates and scientists and behaviorists. But I knew my Owen, and he had his own way of disarming his dissenters. I couldn't place my finger on how he did it, but something about the way he drew people to him—occasionally showing glimpses of brilliance—silenced those who wanted him in the box labeled "special needs." He never acted out and never confronted anybody, but his gentle way of standing his ground with his natural affability was subtly felt by all.

A few months later Owen's teacher sent him home with a book published in 1967 titled *The Outsiders*. I pulled it out of his bag and was amazed that it was their reading assignment because I had never read it, as voracious a reader as I was when I was younger. But then I realized that the movie came out when I was in high school, and at the time, I doubt our schools thought the book was worth studying. Of course, how would you get a teenager to read the book after seeing what was arguably the best proving ground for actors such as Tom Cruise, Emilio Estevez, Patrick Swayze, Ralph Macchio, Rob Lowe, Diane Lane, and Matt Dillon? I suggested to his teacher that we watch the movie and he could do his book report based on that. I thought revisiting a film from my past with my son would be bittersweet, unsure how much he would understand the theme. But it was just the opposite. I found the story was still just as pertinent today as it was then—and the reason they were reading the book in English class. I also recognized yet another way that my son found a workaround for learning. Once again, he was relying on his visual ability to engage, much like the way he learned to swim by watching Michael Phelps. This film gave him an understanding of what that era meant, and he was wholly invested in the theme of the film. He subsequently watched it multiple times, memorizing every line, dressing up for Halloween like Pony Boy, and when he took the verbal test on the film, he scored 100 percent. His teacher was floored, and a begrudging admiration for my son was born.

Chapter Twenty-Nine

I had forgotten how exciting and all-encompassing middle school crushes were. The age of puberty, when hormones begin their wild rush, provoked the most heightened emotions. And Owen was no exception, with or without Down syndrome.

Owen's relationship with Lauren had evolved since second grade. The two of them were almost constant companions at school by the time they graduated. Owen had a way of following Lauren and circling her, but she never seemed to mind. From the day Owen started elementary school on an inclusive campus, I was struck by how he always found his "person." No matter what new school or class we put him in, there was always a girl who saw through his disability and entered his circle. His universe was small, but the vibes that he created made those in it feel special, as if a bit of pixie dust wafted off of Owen and enveloped those who took the time to look for it. First there was Mia, then Samantha. Next came Taylor and then Jane. But Lauren had a way about her that evoked a kindness Owen immediately honed in on and added to his orbit. She was calming to him and took the time to let him know he mattered. Other kids began racing ahead of him in milestones and maturity, but she seemed to hold an invisible hand out to him, as if gesturing, *I'll wait for you.* Because his mom and I both noticed the uniqueness of their relationship, we kept the spark of friendship alive. During the summer, we planned beach days or swim dates so they could hang out. Lauren's family invited him to Dodger baseball games, and the first time they asked, I cringed. I was afraid he couldn't manage. We had never sent him away with another family until now, and I feared he would become separated, or have to use the bathroom and not wash properly. Or worse, they would feel he was a burden. But to my surprise, Owen managed the evening just fine, and Lauren's family continued to invite him again and again, sharing secret jokes between them. There was always a comfort with Owen, as if you could breathe without any pretentiousness or falsehoods. He simply enjoyed people, loved to hug his friends, and was genuinely interested in looking beyond the physical person. I think the people who continued to revolve around Owen understood this; they sensed a calmness when they were in his universe.

I spent years terrified of letting Owen go anywhere without our supervision. When he started school, the very act of allowing him to spend days with other people, even in the safest settings, initially made me panic. I was afraid someone else could never watch him as well as I did. The next scenario was the same, triggering a panicked state until I felt comfortable. While Owen sailed through new scenarios, my guard was constantly up. Dire circumstances floated through my mind. As he got older and was invited out with friends—which didn't happen often, but when it did, I was delighted—my mind would race to envision all the worst-case scenarios and verbally walk through them all with Owen.

"Don't get separated!"

"Watch your step on the stairs so you don't trip."

"Don't comment on someone else's clothes, hair, or looks."

"Don't use the restroom unless her dad goes with you."

"Don't stuff your mouth until you choke."

"And for God's sake, please don't burp, fart, throw up, or otherwise embarrass yourself—or me." It turns out, Lauren's family had so much fun with Owen that there is now a running fart joke from their car ride home that they laugh about constantly.

When middle school started, despite the enormous amount of

kids who spilled out of classrooms to claim lunch tables, Owen and Lauren found each other every day amidst the sea of faces. When I reflect on those days of middle school, my mind always floats to the daily meal they shared together, as if the comfort of friends was somehow the stability he needed in the revolving world of middle school. She loved him for his quirky ways and, as time passed, I heard Owen progress from calling her his friend to referring to her as his girlfriend. She played along, although I took her aside a few times and told her it was okay to be honest with him. He believed fiercely that he would marry Lauren, and I cautioned him again and again that she might find another boyfriend one day. But as I watched him flourish in his new surroundings, I thought about my intentions. Who was I to take that away from him? To stomp on his desires? He would have to manage his own rites of passage, his own expectations. Despite my desire to manage things for him, doing so was not my job anymore. He had graduated into an awakening of his own feelings, and I needed to let him find his way, for better or worse.

As the months unfolded and Owen hit puberty, his affection for Lauren became more apparent. Events held on campus gave me a window into his life. I watched as he hovered around her, his forehead sweaty and suddenly becoming unable to speak to her. I saw a new side of my boy, an emerging man, who was unsure how to proceed, just like any other teenager who is overcome by puberty and awakening hormones. I was caught in indecision about how to manage this. He had every right to fall in love with someone, but we all knew that his disability would be a stopping point for any real relationship with a typical person going forward. I thought of the first time I fell in love in middle school, the ache in my heart when the boy barely acknowledged me, the lover's scenarios I made up in my head. When I graduated to high school, I thought I had put my immature desires away but found myself yet again at the doorstep of a heart-stopping crush, and I faltered under the weight of its seismic magnitude.

I tried to rationalize that Owen was different, and my job was to protect him from insensitive people. But Lauren wasn't that person; she had a goodness that enveloped all of us. My mind wandered daily through the scenarios I was allowing to unfold. What parenting lesson did I need here? And why, for once, couldn't I just let things be? My worry over his life and his evolution was creating a panic mode mentality. Staggering through my days and running stories through my mind, it finally hit me what I was hoping to achieve.

When Owen was a baby, I had one ideal set point in my mind. If he was going to grow up with a mental disability, I was adamant that he would not be the kind of kid who didn't understand parameters. I cringed when I met someone with a disability who shouted his or her name loudly in my ear, or patted my shoulder too hard in greeting. I had a definition in my mind of who I wanted my son to be, and it was as close to normal as possible. To me, these things could be taught. The same parameters I had set for Owen when it came to greeting someone, I also needed to teach him when it came to relationships. Lauren was a willing conspirator. She knew the depths of Owen's emotions for her but never exploited him. She was understanding enough to not trample on his feelings, but instead recognized them and circumvented them. After all, hadn't I fallen in love with all the wrong people during my formative years? The only way we really learn is from experience. She was not going to lead him on, but she would let him be part of her world.

Eighth grade for Owen was the year Lauren had a boyfriend, and that boy became part of their lunchtime group. Owen spoke of him on occasion, but I never heard anger in his voice, or jealousy. The new guy just became another fixture in his daily scenario.

On the eve of Thanksgiving break, the school held football games between grade levels. Kids roamed the outdoors as the band played and cheerleaders stood on the sidelines. Parents were allowed on campus to watch, and in a rare day of chilly autumnal weather, with puffy clouds painting the sky, the games began. I sat on the bench, waiting for Owen's team to show up. We had acquiesced and put him in one class outside of the inclusion model—adaptive PE—and his team was paired up with typical kids to play their games.

Owen's inclusion specialist, Dina, waved at me from across the field, her riotous curls and eclectic fashion identifying her, though she could blend in just as easily with the crowd of teenagers. We had become friends over the course of the year. Her skills in managing Owen's academics and pushing his limitations dovetailed with my expectations. She pushed me, too, with an educator's understanding that the parent's involvement was crucial.

"Hey!" she greeted me. "I saw Owen earlier. He was really upset. He was crying really hard. Tears rolling down his face. When I finally got out of him what he was upset about, he said Lauren broke up with him." This was news to me, and I was afraid of how that scenario went down. I craned my neck trying to see if Owen was lined up with his class for the game.

"I don't know what to think," I said.

"He took it hard," she said. "So whatever's going on, let's hope he can pull out of it."

I spotted Lauren a few bleachers over from me and wandered over. "Hey, Lauren," I said, unsure how she would greet me. In middle school, kids were very vocal in sharing that distance and lack of recognition was the very best kind of parent.

"Oh, hey!" she responded. "Glad you could come!" This was Lauren, though, the girl who always had a kind word for everyone, and her years of being a child actor had given her a maturity that few kids had achieved at this age.

"Can I ask you something? Owen seemed really upset and was crying. I think it has something to do with a breakup?"

"Oh, my boyfriend and I broke up."

"You and Aidan? Not you and Owen? I mean, you know how I feel about that. You don't have to pretend that you and Owen are in a relationship, even though he calls you his girlfriend and is obsessed with you."

She laughed. "I'm not bothered by it. He's sweet. And I do love him."

I slowly walked away. Owen was upset that Aidan and Lauren broke up. How strange was that? I couldn't put the math together, but I knew that when Owen had feelings, he felt them strongly. If he was sad, he was really, really sad and would cry in a deep, sobbing way. Soon enough, he would be over it, as if the depth of his feelings had been worked through and he could move on.

I envied that about Owen—his ability to feel so deeply. He clearly loved deeply, that was apparent, but on the occasions where he had been hurt, or someone had died, he felt it so strongly, as if it encompassed his whole body from his head to his toes. Big fat tears would roll down his face and he would sob, shoulders hunched, the pain wracking his body. Then, when he had moved through the emotion, his sadness dried up. He never forgot those times, and his sorrow, yet it was as if by encountering the grief so strongly, he repaired himself so much faster than I ever could.

Owen's team came out onto the field, and Owen led them, smiling, goading the crowd into cheering for them. In the fifteen minutes they played, he kicked a field goal to great applause. I saw no sign of sadness. When I picked him up from school that day, I asked him about it.

"I was sad, Mom, because Lauren broke up with me."

I corrected him. "No, Owen, she broke up with Aidan, not you."

He turned to me. "Really?" A smile snuck its way onto his face. It didn't erase the sadness he had felt at the time, that was necessary for him, but it gave me a glimpse into the ownership of his feelings and, dare I say it, the mastery.

I mulled this over as I drove him home. He had a way of embracing his emotions, living in the moment—a feat that many of us struggle to do. As old as I was, I had never learned to process my feelings like him, to "feel the feels." Instead, I was always sweeping them under the rug to pull out later. In the meantime, they festered and grew until I was forced to deal with it. Owen had an uncanny ability to process the feeling as they came up, to embrace them and let them go. I was struck by how he never regretted the past or worried about the future. Quite possibly, it's the very reason it wasn't easy for him to learn to tell time, or the days of the week. There was no reason for him to live outside of the moment, and I wondered if that was the intellectual disparity between us, or had he been given a greater gift than I? I couldn't find contentment in any moment, so I chased it day after day.

Chapter Thirty

As I surpassed the half-century mark, my pace slowed. It was hardly noticeable, but my body wasn't as strong, my pace wasn't as fast, and my thoughts didn't track as well. As much as I hated to admit it, I was growing up, too, and growing older. I could embrace the person who I was becoming, or I could chide myself for slowing down and drive myself harder—usually, I chose the latter. But I was tired. I had successfully managed the baby years and toddler years. Now I wanted to pause, to reevaluate. What would give me a better front-row seat to the people my kids were growing into? Managing a full-time job had given me much less visibility into the daily aspects of home life. I resented the pull of work and felt like a ghost in my own home on days that I arrived late and the kids were preparing for bed. I saw how often they turned to their dad with a question, or a thought, or a hug. I knew that the house of cards I so carefully built was about to fall. I needed to extricate myself from the corporate world that had sucked the marrow from me and left an angry shell of a woman. It was time to find a way back to reparation, to building wholeness within. I had ushered my son this far, waging battles as they popped into view, and now it was time to confront my own attackers, to make the space around me safer, happier. I knew it wasn't going to happen overnight, and that was okay. I had watched my son's growth and development track over the years, and despite what seemed an endless road, the milestones came quicker than I thought. Now we were almost to the end of middle school.

I stood in my bathroom, the softly lit mirror reflecting my face, stripped of makeup, flaws obscenely visible. It was nighttime. The kids were downstairs on their multiple devices, sprawled out in what used to be the toy room. It had become a teenager's retreat with pillows strewn everywhere as handmade blankets covered their growing bodies. Their limbs were often intertwined in the way that only siblings who have grown up together can feel comfortable with. The sounds of *Seinfeld* playing in the den, volume turned up, drifted upstairs.

I leaned in closer to the mirror and studied my eyes as if I could find a deeper me locked inside, but the mirror clouded over with my breath. I had always felt like a stranger to myself, and now I recognized even less the face that looked back at me, lined and sallow, no longer sporting a supple glow. I felt unsettled, still at war with what I thought I should look like. Here now, caught in a moment of reflection, I revisited the conversation that made me stop in my tracks and ruminate on who I was and what the future years would look like for our family, for me, and, more specifically, for Owen.

It was one of those random conversations with Dina during middle school when she asked, "Have you thought of what Owen will do after school ends?" I looked at her, half wondering if it was a trick question.

"I have, once in a while. Maybe he can work at Trader Joes? I love that place, and we could get a discount." I laughed uncomfortably. "Although, I haven't seen anyone with a disability working there, unless old age counts."

"No, I mean really thought about it," she said, drawing out the word *really*.

I looked away, frightened by the intensity of her question. I hadn't thought further than where he was at, taking one day at a time, as I had been advised to do when he was a baby. But now, the future loomed close enough that I could almost see it. I could see

Owen reaching into adulthood, becoming a big and strong adult, and it was only a few years away. Suddenly, a sense of panic overtook me. One day he would need more, want more, and I wanted him to grasp for a bigger life than just living at home with his parents. What unnerved me was that I hadn't planned for "more" yet. I hadn't dreamed big enough yet.

"What do you think that's going to look like? The day everyone else starts college, and he is sitting at home, looking at you with an expression that says, 'So, Mom, what are we going to do today?'" she asked.

I gulped. I could see him bounding down the stairs, ready for the day, only to sit on the couch, phone in hand, looking at me with no thought to the future, no motivation to do anything other than watch videos all day long and follow me around, listing his dates combined with memories and peppering it all with, "What's for dinner?"

"That could be my reality," I said, and we both looked at each and started laughing, mine edging on hysteria. I couldn't help myself. She had described exactly what I didn't want to envision.

"I have an idea," she said. "He can take my garbage cans in on Wednesdays. My husband doesn't want to do it when he comes home from a long day. I'll pay him. It will be just like a regular job."

I thought she was joking but quickly realized she meant it. She only lived a few blocks from us, and as I massaged the idea in my head, I realized it might work. We had already tasked him with taking in our garbage cans as his contribution to the family. I could follow him to make sure he did his job correctly, and it would give him something to do. But when I approached Owen about it, he balked.

"I'm not doing it," he said emphatically as I scrambled to figure out how to convince him—since I had already promised Dina.

"Owen, you'll make money. Think about it. You can buy Starbucks for Lauren with all the money you'll be making!" Five dollars a month was barely going to pay for one coffee at Starbucks, but it was my only leverage.

"I promise I'll help you get started." He was silent for a minute, and I could tell he was weighing the odds.

"Okay, fine," he said, with an emphasis on *fine*. "I'll do it. Can I call Lauren and tell her?" He smiled at me, and I was relieved. First hurdle over with. When Owen started his job, I walked the few blocks with him, sorting out his route. As soon as he got the hang of it, he told me to leave, embarrassed that I was following him around. A few weeks went by and Dina called me.

"Hey, there! Marsha, my neighbor across the street, wants to know if Owen can do her cans too." I didn't see a problem with that, and when Owen came home he immediately told me about his second "client."

Within the month, Owen had picked up two new clients—another neighbor of Dina's and our neighbor who lived next door. Like clockwork, every Wednesday after school he would put away his books and lunch bag, then race out the door to take in the garbage cans. Each month, we wrote out receipts to hand out. He came home, pockets brimming with five-dollar bills, and sometimes he would show me an envelope from Marsha with a Starbucks gift card tucked inside.

I was curious about this woman. One afternoon, I told Owen I had to talk to Dina. My real intention was to meet Marsha. As I watched from across the street, Owen methodically took the cans in. He had a very precise way of doing his job; every trash can was handled in a certain order, one by one, and he put them in their places, all perfectly aligned. Then he knocked on her door. I watched as a tiny but mighty-looking woman in her seventies came out of the house, handing Owen an ice-cold water bottle. Then she went to the side of her house and marched up and down, like a general looking at her soldiers, nodding approvingly. As I slowly walked across the street, I heard her say, "Owen, you have done another excellent job for me. Thank you so much for being so considerate and making sure my cans are exactly where they should be."

Owen grinned, covering his mouth in embarrassment at such praise.

I watched, and for a moment I wondered if had I missed a

valuable lesson by not praising Owen so extravagantly before? I had never seen this wide of a grin on his face.

"Excuse me. I wanted to introduce myself. I'm Owen's mom," I said, stepping into her driveway. She barely came up to the top of my shoulders, and her piercing blue eyes captured my gaze. She sized me up for a moment.

"Can I tell you something? I saw this young man one day bringing in Dina's cans, and I was amazed at his attitude. He sings songs while he does his work, he tells stories, and it makes me happy. I asked this fine young man if he could bring my cans in and help me out too." I was a little embarrassed, knowing how loud and off-key Owen sings, and it's always the same One Direction song. I felt as if she was just being nice, so I thanked her and turned away.

She followed me. "One more thing. I'm an acting coach. I work with actors who make millions of dollars. But what makes your son different from them is that he has more self-esteem and confidence than any one of them I have worked with. You are lucky to have him." Her blue eyes held mine for a moment, and I was reminded again of what I knew in my core: I am lucky. We are lucky. All the people who know Owen are lucky to have brushed up against his pure spirit.

Chapter Thirty-One

Marsha's words stayed with me and jolted me into a realization that finally surfaced—even after all my years of therapy. Owen had more self-esteem than I ever had; and he wasn't here to prove anything to anyone. He was taking in dirty, smelly garbage cans with a smile and a song. Who he was would always be enough, yet from the moment he was born, my goal was to make him better, to force him to excel. The irony is that my self-esteem was the one that needed saving, not his. I was trying to prove I was good enough, overcoming every obstacle so that I could hold him up as my trophy. But I was really trying to silence the demons inside me. My son was living his life, step by honest step, no filters, allowing his true nature to be seen as the right people noticed.

I examined my internal beliefs. What was the reflection of myself? For years I had battled my one most vocal critic—Eva. I had always internalized Eva's criticism of me, but I never stopped to think that her words might have been a reflection of her own low self-esteem. Perhaps I was a living, breathing example of what she was afraid to examine within herself. Her contempt for the way I dressed or how I raised my children was apparent. The fact that I chose to have Owen was a direct insult to her belief system. Even if her words were kind, there was usually a barbed insult behind them.

Yet as Owen grew, her view toward his disability softened. His self-esteem was never an issue. He always thought positively of himself and everyone around him. I would often hear him say, "I'm really good at that, aren't I, Mom?" and it may have just been his ability to put in a load of laundry, or make his bed. When he was about ten years old, he began to randomly say, "Today is the best day ever," and it always made me feel good when I happened to be in his vicinity and heard it. Everything he did or said started at a positive level, never dipping into the negative.

He adored his grandmother Eva for reasons I could never quite fathom. He randomly called her to ask how her day was, and I could hear the delight in her voice. His motive was pure, and it wouldn't occur to me until later that perhaps she had never encountered someone who accepted her as fully as he did. Everything in her life was about appearances: how her table was set, how her house was decorated. She even planted winter grass (something I had never heard of growing up in Michigan) so her lawn would look lush in the winter, and forced Erik to plant it at our house too. Her hair and nails were always done, and at Christmas, despite the onset of age, she baked dozens and dozens of Norwegian cookies. If one of them was burned, she threw the batch out and started over.

Over the years, Owen had developed his own quirky obsessions with boy bands, TV shows, dates, and names. Perplexed at this organization of his life, it was not unlike how she managed her life; he had his own set of organization rules too. He cross-referenced everything: birthdates, years, names, and events. When she questioned why he wasn't learning to read, I presented his skill set at memorizing dates and names, and his uncanny ability to recognize a face when I had no context to remember someone.

"That's not going to get him anywhere in life," she said bluntly. But I wasn't so sure she was right anymore. He was organizing his world in the only way he knew how, and somehow, it made sense to him. He talked of our friends across the street named Kim and Chad, and the neighbors behind us named Chad and Jonnelle, and another couple named Joanie and Chad. His visual camera took pictures along the way, so when we passed a man on the street and he said hello, I blanched, scrambling to remember where I knew him from. Yet Owen would come to the rescue with his inordinate way of remembering names and faces, and he would remind me of who the person was as if he were my external memory keeper.

When I told Eva about Owen's job, she snickered. "Garbage cans? That seems appropriate." I clenched my teeth at her sardonic overtones. She was sick now, her body riddled with cancer, yet her disdain was still apparent. Owen loved her even more, despite the decline of her body. When she suffered a slight stroke and stayed with us for a few days, Owen sat on the footstool in front of her, holding her hand.

"You're the most beautiful grandmother in the world," he said as half her face drooped down. I don't know if she could process what he said, but he sat there for hours, regaling her with stories and songs, a captive audience.

I was torn, watching her life slowly fade. She had been the matriarch, the biggest presence in my life for years, and despite being a constant shadow over all of Owen's successes, she still wielded power over my daily decisions. She had held up a mirror to my life for so many years, I wasn't sure what it meant to have to find my own way.

Yet here she sat, her brain littered with tumors, her grandson comforting her. Owen's view of her hadn't changed; he still loved her for exactly who she was. He could see beyond the physical person, and without him being aware of it, he was comforting her soul. This was another lesson from my boy. His ability to see inside and recognize the spirit of a person. He wasn't turned off by the disfigurement the stroke had left, nor was he unwilling to be close to her as her body slowly crumbled and sickness clouded the air with its own distinct smell.

A few weeks later, I came upon Owen practicing a song over and over in the mirror of my closet. "What are you doing?" I asked, curious.

"I'm making up lyrics to a song for Bestamor," he said. When she became a grandmother, she decided to take the Norwegian moniker, Bestamor, rather than the Danish, Farmor, because it had the word "best" in it. Again with the optics.

"Because she's the most beautiful grandma in the world." He smiled, pleased with himself and his secret project.

A few weeks later while she was in hospice, Erik and I took the kids to see her, knowing the end was near. We entered the hospital, the same one Owen had been born in all those years ago. I recognized the elevator and the hallways, and memories of his birth and his time in the NICU besieged me, like ghosts walking the halls. I wanted to reach out to that scared girl I was, to congratulate her on the birth of her baby, and tell her everything would be okay. But the memories were too rich for me to handle right now, too laden with emotion. The irony was not lost on me that we welcomed Owen's first breath in this place where Eva would take her last.

She was in the hospice wing, unconscious, mouth open, breath even. Her body showed signs of decay, and her hair that she had always prided herself on lay in wisps of faded grey, limp on the bed. Tess and Axel sat in the corner, shy in the face of death. But not Owen. He walked over to her side and leaned in as close as he could.

"This one's for you, Bestamor," he said, then proceeded to sing the lyrics he had made up to the tune of a One Direction song. His off-kilter voice crooned the words, "Cuz you're the best grandma in the world," followed by "the only one in the world."

Her even breathing suddenly caught, and she gasped. Erik and I looked at each other, and I felt the hairs on my arms rise, certain it was her way of acknowledging him. His song faded, and he leaned in as close as he could, unfazed by her skeletal look. He had said his goodbye in his own eclectic way.

It occurred to me that perhaps Owen was here for both of us, Eva and me, to show us that it wasn't about loving the external person, the visual carriage we lived our life through; it was about seeing into the soul and the spirit within. Only Owen had eyes for that, and despite his visual impairment since he was two, he could see further into a person's core than those of us with 20/20 vision.

Owen opened my eyes to a different way of looking at my life, at what surrounded me, than I had thought possible.

With the passing of Eva, I let go of the stringent boundaries I put on myself. I stopped looking at the negative in the mirror and challenged myself to find a hint of positive in the reflection staring back at me. I was finally ready to step into the person I knew I could be. I was finally going to trust my instinct and explore the path to becoming a writer, which I had set aside for so many decades to be the breadwinner, to champion Owen and to raise my kids the best way I knew how.

Chapter Thirty-Two

I think hard and try to recall what days were like before I had kids, before my time was swept into the vortex of motherhood. What did I do? Where did I go? What was it like to have a span of time that was mine alone? How could I have ever treated time with such negligence, with the assumption that it would always be there for me to wrap myself in? Time passed in a hurry, more ruthlessly than I gave it credit for.

I revisited the questions I thought about when my kids were babies: Who will I be when my kids grow up? Will I be the kind of woman I can be proud of? The kind of woman who went to battle when it was necessary and even when it was not? Will I be okay with looking back on my life as I enter the sunset years and know that every experience—the good, the bad, and the not-so-good—was worth it? Will I like what I see?

A woman beckons from the half-formed dreams of my past. She is me, a shadowy figure of the girl I was, not the woman I have become. She is young and selfish, determined and naive. She lives life powered by goals. She forges ahead on her path, a belief in destiny. She is unaware that her story will be more than she ever dreamed of, and far different than she can imagine.

When my kids were little, we had friends with older children.

"Just wait until they start school. It will change your life," they all said, as if it was an invitation to a secret club. But it didn't change my life in the way I thought it would. I didn't experience this great freedom. In fact, starting school meant the world was encroaching on our simple lives, and the language became new again, something I wasn't prepared for. There was a system that played out, etiquette of play dates and birthday parties and after-school activities. I felt as if someone had handed me a computer and asked me to code software. I was out of my element. I was that parent who wanted my kids to stay little, to be here when I got home, to take their time growing up.

But "Mommy" turned into "Mom," and their bones lengthened, their vocabulary expanded, and their minds stretched. My two younger ones pushed me away as they grew, their invisible hands creating a barrier to prevent me from walking next to them. The eye rolls and the head-turning taught me my place in their world. I felt as if I was always training them, disciplining them, teaching them. My smile only came as a reward on some days. I was militant in my thoughts that I want them—no, I *need* them—to be good, responsible citizens one day. That day draws nearer and nearer. The disciplinarian I am frightens me sometimes, and I wonder if I am pushing them away, making them grow up faster.

By the time high school arrived for Owen, I was no longer straddling different worlds. They had all melded into a series of beginnings and endings. Summer morphed into fall, then faded into winter. The comforting years of elementary school were over, and I watched as my children grew in new directions, pressing forward into life faster than I was ready for. A melancholy took over as I mourned the loss of the baby days, which, in retrospect, seemed easier than perhaps they were. I watched as humans emerged and now, despite the fleeing of time, I can only bend and shape what is left. The fragments of the little ones they once were are buried deeper now, and I find myself scrutinizing them, wishing I could pull out the cherubic smiles and chubby hands, the astute observations and lisped words just one more time. They are like lost treasures, buried within the landscape of my mind. I get caught staring at them, and they ask, "What?" in their now self-conscious ways. My reverie breaks and I am hurtled back into the present.

I am lost in an upheaval of my work life, one I hadn't prepared for and didn't anticipate, yet welcome all the same. After years of holding a corporate job, and amidst a power grab for those hungry enough to pursue it, I was left in the crossfire—wounded, angry, and dismissed. The stinging resentment prodded me to manipulate what little power I had left, and I seized the opportunity to make the company pay me to leave. I am now untethered, and for the first time in my life, I'm unwilling to throw myself back into the race and valiantly battle to find another job. I look around me and breathe in the daily life that was always there but never mine to inhabit. There is no place I want to be anymore, no desk I want to sit at, no career option I want to pursue. Bitterness stings my tongue slightly as I slip into the cloak of not belonging anymore; no business cards to identify my owner, but also no timekeeper to steal the hours of my day. My time is now my own, and I disrupt the thoughts of failure as I set out to build my own business model. I am a consultant now, the nom de plume for anyone with decades of skill but a nomad in business.

My kids have all moved on to the next phase where my presence is not required visually, but imperceptibly.

"Drop me off at the corner, Mom," said Tess as she fiddled with her ever-shorter uniform skirt, her legs lengthening daily.

"I'll meet you at the pizza place," Axel said. I spy him and his friends chumming it up in the parking lot, an ease of years between the group belies the newness of middle school. I am not welcome in the halls, or on the field, or anywhere that they have to acknowledge me. I know this is normal, but after Owen's willingness to hold my hand through the years, running up to me during lunchtime with a mighty hug, I am saddened by the distancing that they—and I—must learn.

Chapter Thirty-Three

It is December, and Owen's high school is hosting a winter ball. I told Owen he must go, even though Lauren cannot attend because she has to be at her best friend's birthday party. He told me no, he's not going, not without Lauren. He was adamant about it. For the first time, I saw a moroseness I had never seen before. He has escalated his awareness to the level of a typical high school kid. He is not going to a dance without Lauren.

"I'm just going to sit home with no plans. Everyone else has plans, but I don't care. I'm just going to stay home," he muttered loudly enough for me to hear.

I marched over to him. "Look at me. You are not going to sit home. You are in tenth grade, and this dance is for you. I will not allow you to spend your high school years sitting on the couch." I was insistent. Owen knows I always mean business.

"Mom, why should I go when Lauren can't? She's my girl." This time, I understand. It's high school, and he may not be typical, but he has studied typical kids so intently that he is aware of the intricacies of high school relationships.

"Guess what? When I was in high school, I went to dances without a boyfriend. That's what you do; you go anyway. Maybe you'll be miserable, but maybe you'll have fun. You won't know unless you try." He looked at me, seconds ticking by.

"Okay, fine. I'll do it. I'll try." I was relieved. The dance was held at the Los Angeles Zoo. When we arrived, we were both awed by the magical glory of holiday lights strung throughout the area. We were early, so I got Owen a plate of food and sat him at a table. Even as I did that, I became aware of kids streaming in, two by two, groups of them, dazzling in their finery. He ate, head down, not looking at anything or anyone, and for a few seconds I wondered if I had made a big mistake by hauling him to a dance where nobody understood him. I wanted to grab him and run as fast as I could, dash out of the most typical high school experience I could ever ask for and that I had goaded him into attending. As the kids sidled up to the buffet table for food, one of them saw Owen and sat down next to him. It was a boy who had broken up with his girlfriend, a couple Owen had studied for months, watching them as they kissed on the afternoon bus ride home. Neither of the boys spoke; just gave a fist bump and a glance, but I felt silent words pass between them. They understood each other: two boys without their girls.

As the night went on, the kids danced, and when I walked around to find Owen, he was sitting with a few guys, slumped in chairs, hands in their pockets, all without dates, all "hanging out." It was late when we left the dance. The crowds had cleared and the massive light displays were turned off one by one. We walked slowly to our car, an eerie feeling of animals hidden, yet watching us.

"Did you have fun, Owen?" I asked.

"Yes, Mom, I did." He put his arm around me as we walked, and I sensed that he, too, would begin to separate from me, to find his own way, and I wouldn't need to be his puppeteer forever.

Why was I so driven to help him succeed? Why not? Years ago when I was in college, I had gone with some friends on a lark to a nunnery for the weekend to consider the contemplative life. The defining moment for me happened late on Saturday afternoon. I took a few minutes to read and found myself in a room filled with sunlight, cots lined up against the walls in anticipation of summer camps. I sat in a rocking chair, embracing the stillness. Words rustled around me, and I heard a voice: "I have a bigger plan for you. You can't stay here; it won't ever be enough for you."

On Sunday, when I unpacked my suitcase, a piece of paper fluttered out of the information packet they had given us. On it were the simple words written by Malcolm X: "If not now, then when? If not me, then who?"

Those words returned to dance in my brain. I had put off defining who I was for so many years, a deferral of sorts, and Owen was another shield for me to place in between me and my life. I could hide behind the "special needs mom" label whenever it suited me, but inevitably, I had to come face-to-face with the ageless moniker that becoming a mom forces you into. I had inexplicably become a warrior, my invisible weapons tucked neatly inside me. I had not chosen my path as a parent of a child with special needs, but long ago, the voice that whispered to me must have known my future was already written, and it was not going to be lived in a tiny town in Michigan. My future contained a longer, bolder road that I had to travel, wrong turns and dead ends and all. The day I got pregnant and knew I would never test for any chromosomal abnormalities was the day I said yes to that bigger life, to the path that I trod.

At every juncture, I sense a fork in the road between Owen and a typical child's path, and it is my opportunity to be his guidance counselor. My other two kids have pushed me away as much as they could, finding their own tribe and gently dipping their toes in the big lake of trial and error. Not Owen. He still hugs me daily and calls me his "beautiful mama," proud to walk with his hand in mine in public. He accepted my interference, my pop-up way stations of new adventures to add to his life's experiences. Was I wrong for still wanting to steer the boat for him? I watched him succeed in the engagement of others, and he is emerging from boyhood into the inkling of adulthood. I feel as if I am writing my own handbook based on the belief that "life will not be a special needs class." Owen must learn to live and work in society as we do, albeit his own, more loosely defined place.

A few years from now, mandatory school will be over and the

light at the end of the tunnel will beckon. Or is that tunnel just the start of another path? When will I have the courage to let Owen go and find his own way? What I thought would be different for him is actually the same. We are all supporting our kids as they reach into the world in their own unique way, and we all want them to have the same set of survival skills. I want him to find his own survival skills. The set of tools I give him may look different, but the platform from which he will jump is one I have created, and I can only hope it's stable as a rock.

Owen and I have talked about college as a real possibility. He has a friend with Down syndrome attending Fresno State, which has a program for adults with disabilities. As for as long as I can remember, I've had my eye on UCLA's program. I never stop planning, my mind is constantly looking for the next thing for him because I know the instructions that other kids follow will never be his road map. I must create a new road map for him, as I have always done. He has a right to the same kind of life as anyone else, and maybe that's why I try so hard to find it for him, to give him direction. We all need guidance and direction, right? Without others to go before us, we are all lost.

As a parent, I have expanded within myself a thousand times, repeating the same scenarios but adding nuances, turning experiences into pivotal moments that defined my life. I have always needed definition in my life. It is in my nature to put words to what I do; there has to be a pattern and rules for it to make sense to me—not unlike Owen's way of life. He has lived his own particular set of rules that defy convention and veer from the norm. There are times I smiled to myself when I heard him drop a line, or shared an observation, and it rang truer than most of what I heard throughout my day from business executives and wise friends. When I made mistakes and berated myself for them, my other two kids looked at me and crept away. Not Owen. He sidled up to me and wrapped me in a hug, a wordless gesture of comfort.

"We all make mistakes, Mama. You're not alone." The simple lines he fed me made me stop and pivot. My seventeen-year-old boy forgave me over and over, even after I got upset at him for not listening to me, or he asked incessantly, "Are you mad? Are you mad? Are you mad?" Which usually happened when I said, "Hurry up! Come on! It's time to go." Owen has his own internal clock, for which there is no precision, and he moves accordingly. He is ready when he is ready, and I've struggled to allow him to be that way. Perhaps it was because I struggled with control—over myself, over my life, and over Owen.

His power of observation goes unnoticed by most people. It's the reason he has been successful in school: his precise notation of how things are done translates into the exact same intonation of speech or pattern of movement. I sometimes wished I had that superpower, but mine is different. If you had asked me when my kids were little if my superpower was being a mom, I would have given you a frazzled, cynical look. *I am just trying to survive over here,* my look would say. It took me a while to gaze at myself with kind eyes and say, "Yes, I am a good mom. My superpower is my patience, my ability to stand back and let a scenario unfold, waiting for the right moment to take a stand and define the outcome."

I often think I resided in a space of tentative optimism about how I defined myself as a mother. Owen is slowly opening up the gates of freedom to allow that optimism to flow. If someone were to ask me on a spiritual level why Owen was born to me, I would answer immediately that he was sent to be my teacher, my Buddha. The Buddha is defined as "one who is truly awake." This definition made me pause. As I sorted through my life and what I concluded about it, I know for sure that I am not "truly awake." But Owen is. One Christmas, when Owen was twelve, he said, "Mommy, I have the best Christmas present ever for you."

"Oh, yeah? What is it?"

"I love you! That's my Christmas present." At the same time, my other two kids were clamoring for Barbie dolls and trucks, games and markers, stickers and candy. Owen simply understood that amidst all the craziness of having to fulfill the physical gift-giving, he gave me a present that needed no bows or wrapping paper. It was simply the gift of love. How thoughtful was that for a twelve-year-old?

Owen's way of moving through the world has always been

something I aspire to. He is "truly awake." The Buddhist beliefs are centered on the idea of being attentive and aware of the here and now. When I was working full-time, I spent my days and nights rushing around, planning events both professionally and personally. My mind was always on the future rather than the present. Cynthia and I joked that we lived our lives in the future-present because that's when our events took place. Owen has perfected living in the moment, and his ability to be content is what strikes me most. He doesn't stress over the past, and he won't think about tomorrow because it's not here yet. I used to worry that he would never learn the days of the week because yesterday and tomorrow made no sense to him. These days, he understands the concept of what day his job is on, or when his acting class is, but I have never seen him anxious about the past or the future. In the present moment it doesn't matter; it just is.

Chapter Thirty-Four

I remember a time when my kids were little, and going to the zoo was a regular outing. We walked around, stopping to look at the new gorilla exhibit, which was always crowded. My kids stood next to me on their tip toes, craning their little necks to see. Behind me, a woman pushed a child in a wheelchair, trying to get through. She slowly inched the wheelchair forward as I heard her apologies. "Sorry, sorry."

I recognized this woman; I once was her. We are the parents of kids with special needs who began with apologies, as we so carefully traversed our worlds, afraid of attracting too much attention to our child. We wheeled them through life, making amends, as if it's not enough to feel as if we have already offended society with a child who isn't the norm, now we must apologize as we navigate through it. We tried not to draw attention, even as we have been gifted with an attention-getting individual, one who will remind us to question and participate in life. We softly apologized and briskly carried on, and only I understood the true badge of courage that that the brave mother wore and carried forward in her every day battle.

Along the way, I stopped apologizing, whether I no longer felt sorry for myself or sorry for my son, I'm not sure. Either way, it doesn't matter. To apologize continuously was to admit that there was an error; that something was not okay. I know now that is the complete opposite of where I stand today. I have encountered more compassion, more faith, and more love in my life with my son as he showed me the depths of my emotions. I didn't get to take a break from my work with him; it was relentless, persistent, and all-encompassing. Sound familiar? Because it is. Because any mother will tell you that the lessons you learned become the gift. It is the inherent nature of a mother to fight for her child, to take up the sword, to go to battle in the name of love. We have all carried the torch for our children because it's not just my child who has special needs, it's my friend's child, my sister's child, my cousin's child, and children all over the world who, if we really look, have special needs. Children are special, and children have needs; we can all see the equation and solve the problem.

According to *Merriam-Webster*, a fairy tale is a story marked by seemingly unreal beauty, perfection, luck, or happiness. A few years ago, I went in to say goodnight to Owen, his face softening as sleep took over. Turning to leave, he called out, "Mom, thank you for everything you do for me and Tess and Axel. You make it magical."

This is my fairy tale. So how do I write my happy ending? Perhaps there is no ending, just as there was no beginning. I was living my life, and Owen was born to us, and other people will come into his life, and eventually I will exit his life. The beginning will have no end. A few nights ago, as Owen was getting ready for bed, he said to me, "Mom, I'll just put this out there, for the future . . ."

"Mm-hmm. What's that?" I asked, half-listening as I read a book.

"I love you. That will always be your future." I stopped for a moment, thinking he had gotten the structure of what he was trying to say mixed up. I analyzed his words, rolling them around in my mind. But he hadn't gotten anything wrong. He was perfectly right. He had told me what he knows to be true, now and forever.

Epilogue

When we began the journey of inclusion for our son, I had no idea what it would look like or how the incremental event and experiences would shape him and me. Given that Owen had been fully included since second grade, it was a testimony to how much he exceeded our expectations (and the expectation of others) when we hosted his eighteenth birthday party in Malibu the summer before his senior year, where we were living temporarily until our house remodel was finished. For the last eleven years, since second grade, we have hosted a birthday party with the same group of typical kids he knew from school. Because it was held during summer, it always felt like a reunion of sorts. When the kids graduated from elementary school, the reunions became more poignant as they sailed through middle school, and then even more so as they spread out to different high schools. Owen's birthday always remained a highlight at the end of June. This particular birthday, we had begun to surface from the isolation of COVID, and his friends were eager to meet up again. All the kids who came were about to enter their senior year, but because we held Owen back one year, he was reaching this milestone before any of them. It didn't matter. They still gathered to laugh and reminisce.

We all walked down to the ocean to catch the sunset as the giant golden orb dropped beyond the horizon, trailing cotton-candy pink and blue streaks across the sky. The kids laughed and danced in the sand, taking selfies with each other. That day is forever etched in my mind, especially the moment when Owen gave Lauren a tender hug under the waning colors of the sky. Back at the house, the kids took blankets and walked to the end of the field to see if they could find the Milky Way in the inky blackness. Peals of laughter drowned out the crash of waves as the adults drank wine and soaked up the first blush of freedom from COVID and the last days of childhood that our kids were about to leave behind. Senior year was around the corner, and most of them would be off to college by the following summer. As I watched the evening unfold, a quiet sense of pride took hold of me. I helped create this. I had nurtured this. But I wasn't done yet; there was still more to do.

As summer ended and we enrolled our kids in their new school, I had another IEP for Owen's transfer. The first thing they mentioned was that the district doesn't support full inclusion, so it was off the table. (I already knew that. I had done my research, as always).

"That's fine. I just want him to have an amazing senior year, full of all the same pomp and circumstance the other seniors will have."

As Owen integrated himself into the school year, the first thing he did was leave class at the lunch bell and go find a spot in the middle of campus, firmly cementing his desire to be among typical kids.

His teacher caught up with me after school and said, "He can't do that. He can't just leave the classroom."

I was puzzled. "It's a free period, right? Everyone gets to choose where they want to eat their lunch."

"But he is my responsibility. What if something happens?" she responded.

I laughed. "He just wants to choose where he sits for lunch. If I have to get that written into his IEP, then let's have a meeting." I had forgotten how any tiny change had to be discussed and documented, unlike when he was in full inclusion.

As the days fell into each other, the teachers understood more and more how capable he was, learning the layout of campus within a week. He obeyed the rules, but he always wanted his freedom. I understood this because we had given him a taste for it with each passing year: the sleepaway camps, walking to school, then taking the bus in high school with typical kids, or waiting on campus by himself for us to pick him up. So many tiny opportunities inched Owen toward freedom, and this opened the door to the lure of independence.

That spring, after encouragement from his teacher, he tried out and made the varsity swim team. I pulled away more and more each practice: dropping him off, then having him walk from the corner, then asking another parent to take him. Each was a test of his ability to be more independent. Some of his peers volunteered to make sure he got on the bus on time for swim meets, and he managed to change, put on sunscreen, and (almost) read the race boards. I noticed a camaraderie that enveloped him as he folded himself into the chaos of the swim meets. I was proud of Owen, even though he came in last at every race. Despite that, he would get out of the pool and say, "I did good, Mom, didn't I?" with a big grin pasted on his face. At the last swim meet, the final race for Owen was a relay, which he had done a few times before, and despite their best effort, his team always came in last. When I circled back to find Owen after the race, I saw the other three boys and thanked them for being so kind to him.

"I know he was the slowest on the team," I said hesitantly.

"I liked having him on our team. He's funny," one of the boys replied as he toweled off. The tallest boy, who stood well over six feet tall and dwarfed Owen, looked me in the eye and said, "I'm recovering from back surgery. I came to my races with the best I could offer. We all swim our own race." I was grateful that they understood. And I was assured again that this is what Owen's life would be like going forward. There will always be people who find him and understand him.

I sit with my son as he painstakingly types words on my computer with his fingers, gently urging him to use two hands. I itch to take over for him, to do it for him, but I can't. This is his application to a four-year residential college program. He already attends a junior college a few times a week: classes designed especially for kids with a certificate of completion rather than a diploma. The classes are computer-based, and instructions happen at a much slower pace. But I see the growth of his knowledge as he strides onto campus among other typical kids and walks to his first class. Did I ever dream he would be accessing his future like this? Did I ever dare to dream bigger? To find the research that supports his independence in this manner? After stumbling onto the website thinkcollege.net (a resource of colleges throughout the US that have programs for adults with disabilities), it had never occurred to me that there was a possibility of Owen moving away, stepping into a bigger world than I could imagine. But here we are, snuggled together on my bed as he pulls up his application. The questions are simplified, and he reads them slowly, mouthing each word as he does. As he studies the words with intense concentration, I watch him. I note the perfectly stenciled eyebrows (God-given to kids with Down syndrome), the small ears with a lightly creased fold in them, and the erratic beard growing with wiry hairs sticking out in the places he didn't shave close enough. Yet he always remembers to clean up his mustache "so the ladies will like it, Mom." Owen tells me this after his ritualistic pattern of grooming.

"What's this word, Mom?"

"That's *hygiene*," I reply.

"The question is, do I have good hygiene that I can manage on my own?" he reads with precision. I explain what hygiene is: taking showers, washing his face, brushing his teeth.

"Oh, that's an easy one," he replies. "I'm a good hygiene manager." I smile, but not because of how he framed it. I smile because he used the word *manager*. Was there a time in my life that I didn't think he would ever *manage*? Absolutely. During the early years, I sometimes looked at him with sadness, thinking he would never manage his life like typical kids. As he got older, that word often described my life as I managed three kids and a full-time job. And there were days I sometimes didn't think I could manage.

"What's so funny, Mom?" he asks as a smile plays at the corners of his lips. He always wants in on the joke. I tell him it's nothing while holding tight to the inkling of truth that when he gets into college, he will learn to manage in situations far away from me, and he will manage to be the best version of who he is.

Acknowledgments

There are so many people who have come into my life and made an impact from the moment my son was diagnosed; people who I otherwise might not have met. I started writing this book when Owen was only a year old, based on a daily journal I began when I was five weeks pregnant. Oh, the foresight to capture what I didn't know would be this extraordinary adventure! But it took many, many years ignoring the call to continue until by chance, I met Kim O'Hara, who was able to do what I never could: coax the structure and outline out of me until it began to take on the shape of a memoir. Thank you, Judy and Anne at Aristata Press, for believing my story is worth telling. To the best editor I could hope for, Jenna Love-Schrader, I would never have been able to edit my work the way you did: thoughtfully and meticulously.

To my beta readers, who I owe a deep debt of gratitude to for taking the time to read my book when we all have so much going on in our lives: Kristine Shahine, Angela Mickunas, Dina Marie Swann, Kathryn Trainor, Laura Wagner, Patricia Hass, Anne Lewis, and Malin Svensson. (I would mention my husband here, but he couldn't get through it all because he was overcome with emotion). To my amazingly talented friend Lisa Thomas, who designed the cover.

To the moms who joined me in this club over the past years, I cannot thank you enough for letting me be part of your journey as we walked this new path. There is not one among you who I have not found to be a courageous, fierce mama who only wants the best for our kids.

To the many friends, therapists, teachers, and kind strangers who lifted me up when I was down and showed me the beauty in the life I was living. Each of you gave me the courage to get up and try again.

To our families, who rallied with us when Owen was born and always said yes to being a part of our journey. To my sisters Anne, Marie and Celeste, I could not have asked for better best friends.

To those who weren't mentioned in this book but were a part of our lives, it's because I simply could not include every story. Know that I treasure and value all of you, and each of you has contributed in helping me raise this extraordinary boy.

To quote Ram Dass, "We're all just walking each other home." Thank you for walking this journey with me.

About the Author

Suzanne Lezotte grew up in Redford, Michigan, with eight brothers and sisters. Known as the bookworm of the family, she had read *Gone with the Wind* twice by the time she started high school. Her love of words led to a degree in English from Western Michigan University, and after graduation she moved to Los Angeles. She spent the last twenty years working in the entertainment tech space as an executive and journalist. The COVID lockdown gave her the opportunity to finally write her memoir, and an essay from a chapter in her book garnered an Honorable Mention in the 2022 Writer's Digest contest. She lives in Westlake Village with her husband and three kids.

You can read more about her life with Owen on her website, suzannelezotte.com

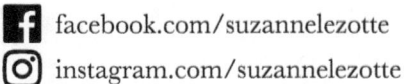

facebook.com/suzannelezotte
instagram.com/suzannelezotte

Select Aristata Press Titles

LEAVINGS: Memoir of a 1920s Hollywood Love Child, by Megan McClard, 2022

Spanish language edition of: *Tell Mother I'm in Paradise: Memoirs of a Political Prisoner in El Salvador* by Ana Margarita Gasteazoro—*Díganle a mi madre que estoy en el paraíso: Memorias de una prisionera política en El Salvador*, Edited by Judy Blankenship and Andrew Wilson, 2022.

Coming in 2023

This Rough Magic: At Home on the Columbia Slough, by Nancy Henry and Bruce Campbell, illustrated by Amanda Williams, August 2023.

Butterfly Dreams: a Novel, by Anne McClard, September 2023.

Women Caught in the Crossfire: One Woman's Quest for Peace in South Sudan, by Abuk Jervis Makuac and Susan Lynn Clark, October 2023.

Aristata Press is non-profit organization. We depend on charitable contributions and volunteers to keep the lights on. We are a tax exempt 501(c)(3) organization (EIN 92-0281706), which means that your contributions are tax deductible. Contributions that we receive will go directly to supporting the publications of deserving literary works by authors that for one reason or another would be unlikely to find a home in the for-profit publishing sector.

Please visit us at: https://aristatapress.com

www.ingramcontent.com/pod-product-compliance
Lightning Source LLC
Chambersburg PA
CBHW020656060526
44119CB00090B/410/J